Cambridge Elements ≡

Elements in the Politics of Development
edited by
Rachel Beatty Riedl
Einaudi Center for International Studies and Cornell University
Ben Ross Schneider
Massachusetts Institute of Technology

Mario Einaudi
CENTER FOR
INTERNATIONAL STUDIES

 MIT CENTER FOR INTERNATIONAL STUDIES

CRIMINAL POLITICS AND BOTCHED DEVELOPMENT IN CONTEMPORARY LATIN AMERICA

Andreas E. Feldmann
University of Illinois Chicago
Juan Pablo Luna
Pontificia Universidad Católica de Chile

 CAMBRIDGE
UNIVERSITY PRESS

Shaftesbury Road, Cambridge CB2 8EA, United Kingdom

One Liberty Plaza, 20th Floor, New York, NY 10006, USA

477 Williamstown Road, Port Melbourne, VIC 3207, Australia

314–321, 3rd Floor, Plot 3, Splendor Forum, Jasola District Centre, New Delhi – 110025, India

103 Penang Road, #05–06/07, Visioncrest Commercial, Singapore 238467

Cambridge University Press is part of Cambridge University Press & Assessment, a department of the University of Cambridge.

We share the University's mission to contribute to society through the pursuit of education, learning and research at the highest international levels of excellence.

www.cambridge.org
Information on this title: www.cambridge.org/9781108958059

DOI: 10.1017/9781108955461

First published 2023

A catalogue record for this publication is available from the British Library.

ISBN 978-1-108-95805-9 Paperback
ISSN 2515-1584 (online)
ISSN 2515-1576 (print)

Additional resources for this publication at www.cambridge.org/feldmann.

Criminal Politics and Botched Development in Contemporary Latin America

Elements in the Politics of Development

DOI: 10.1017/9781108955461
First published online: June 2023

Andreas E. Feldmann
University of Illinois Chicago

Juan Pablo Luna
Pontificia Universidad Católica de Chile

Author for correspondence: Andreas E. Feldmann, feldmana@uic.edu

Abstract: This Element investigates the relationship between the narcotics industry and politics and assesses how it influences domestic political dynamics, including economic development prospects in Latin America. It argues that links between criminal organizations, politicians, and state agents give rise to criminal politics (i.e., the interrelated activity of politicians, organized crime actors, and state agents in pursuing their respective agendas and goals). Criminal politics is upending how countries function politically and, consequently, impacting the prospects and nature of their social and economic development. The Element claims that diverse manifestations of criminal politics arise depending on how different phases of drug-trafficking activity (e.g., production, trafficking, and money laundering) interact with countries' distinct politico-institutional endowments. The argument is probed through the systematic examination of four cases that have received scant attention in the specialized literature: Chile, Paraguay, Peru, and Uruguay.

Keywords: drug trafficking, criminal politics, development, Latin America, corruption

ISBNs: 9781108958059 (PB), 9781108955461 (OC)
ISSNs: 2515-1584 (online), 2515-1576 (print)

Contents

Further online supplementary material for appendix can be accessed at Cambridge.org/Feldmann/Luna

1 Introduction

In March 2022, Paraguayan law enforcement agents carried out the most significant drug operation in the country's history, dismantling a vast criminal ring linked to former President Horacio Cartes who ruled Paraguay between 2013 and 2018 (Rainsford and Saffon 2022). The efficacy of operation A Ultranza PY, as it came to be known, puzzled most observers because, in the notoriously opaque Paraguayan context, such raids were unprecedented. This operation was only made possible because of a dispute between two factions of the country's perennial ruling party, the Colorado Party. The dispute pitted Cartes against current President Mario Abdó; the two became embroiled in a major power struggle in which Abdó temporarilly prevailed.

Beyond revealing how drug trafficking permeates the highest political echelons of the Paraguayan political system, the operation unearthed a vast transnational web of corruption with ramifications across the region. This became apparent following the tragic assassination of Marcelo Pecci, a Paraguayan prosecutor in charge of operation A Ultranza PY who was killed while on his honeymoon in Colombia. The murder, carried out by local hitmen, was allegedly ordered by the Uruguayan drug trafficker Sebastián Marset. Marset had previously been prosecuted in Uruguay for his association with a criminal network linked to the Cartes family and Fahd Jamil, a Brazilian drug trafficker who is one of the most influential figures in the Paraguayan criminal underworld. Jamil and Cartes operated several profitable macro-trafficking routes to export drugs from Paraguay to neighboring countries, Europe, and Asia (Dalby 2022).[1] Their business flourished during the administration of Andrés Rodríguez, the son-in-law of General Alfredo Strössner who, in 1989, became Paraguay's first democratically elected president (1989–93).

Marset was briefly detained in Dubai for entering the country with a fake passport after he fled Paraguay, but he used contacts in the Uruguayan government to procure a legitimate Uruguayan passport and evade justice. Cartes' operation also included important links with legitimate businesses, including one of the top Chilean corporations with whom he developed a partnership to distribute gasoline and produce beer and soft drinks (Sepúveda and ABC Color 2022). Notwithstanding his legal problems, Cartes was elected leader of Paraguay's Colorado Party in December 2022, and his political protégée, Santiago Peña, won the country's presidential election by a wide margin on April 30, 2023.

---

[1] Within trafficking, we distinguish *macro-trafficking*, which refers to a large transnational operation involving powerful drug-trafficking organizations (DTOs), and *micro-trafficking*, which involves smaller operations and less sophisticated groups.

This vignette, resembling something from a Hollywood movie, describes the intricate connections between different forms of organized crime linked to drug trafficking, the business sector, and high-ranking politicians in contemporary Latin America.[2] As the story highlights, the lurking power of the drug trade is deeply impacting societies and has entered the bloodstream of many political systems, reaching the highest echelons of power (Bergman 2018a). Notwithstanding differences among countries, drug trafficking has become pervasive, fueling problems ranging from institutional corruption and social upheaval to violence and democratic erosion (Arias and Goldstein 2010; Davis 2006). Indeed, Latin America displays disconcerting levels of equifinality (Feldmann and Luna 2022) in countries that vary in institutional capacity and economic development, the illicit drug industry has led to challenges in several dimensions, including the rule of law (Méndez, O'Donnell, and Pinheiro 1996), security and governance (Albarracín and Barnes 2020), and democracy (Trejo and Ley 2017).

This Element investigates the relationship between the narcotics industry and politics, and assesses how this relationship influences existing political dynamics at the national level in Latin America.[3] We argue that this connection is engendering what we conceptualize as *criminal politics*, by which we mean the interrelated activity of politicians, organized crime actors, and state agents in pursuing their respective agendas and goals (economic, political, personal). Criminal politics is upending traditional dynamics, changing how countries function politically and, consequently, impacting the prospects and nature of their social and economic development. We also claim that diverse

---

[2] Organized crime is a contested term and definitions of it abound. Reuter (2009) defines it in terms of private firms operating illicit markets, whereas Albanese (2000) describes it as "continuing criminal enterprise that rationally works to profit from illicit activities; its continuing existence is maintained through the use of force, threats, monopoly control, and/or the corruption of public officials" (p. 411). Lupsha (1983), for his part, indicates that

> organized crime is an activity, by a group of individuals, who consciously develop task roles and specializations, patterns of interaction, statuses, and relationships, spheres of accountability and responsibilities; and who with continuity over time engage in acts legal and illegal usually involving (a) large amounts of capital, (b) buffers (nonmember associates), (c) the use of violence or the threat of violence (actual or perceived), (d) the corruption of public officials, their agents, or those in positions of responsibility and trust. This activity is goal oriented and develops sequentially over time. Its purpose is the accumulation of large sums of capital and influence, along with minimization of risk. Capital acquired (black untaxed monies) are in part processed (laundered) into legitimate sectors of the economy through the use of multiple fronts and buffers to the end of increased influence, power, capital and enhanced potential for criminal gain with increasingly minimized risk. (pp. 60–61)

For further definitions, see Varese (2017).

[3] While our discussion centers on the role of narcotics, its theoretical underpinnings apply to other illicit activities. Hereafter, when we use the term "criminal organization," we refer to diverse forms of organized crime linked to drug trafficking.

manifestations of criminal politics arise, depending on how different phases of drug-trafficking activity (production, trafficking, and money laundering) interact with countries' distinct politico-institutional endowments. Criminal politics, we posit, surfaces in territorial arenas, where most of the literature has concentrated. However, criminal politics also characterizes functional arenas (transportation sites, customs, real estate, finance), where the relevance of criminal influence in politics is less visible and harder to track, but also highly consequential. By simultaneously focusing on territorial and functional arenas, we can scale up the analysis from local, often marginal communities to national and international levels.[4]

We probe our argument by examining four countries: Paraguay, Peru, Chile, and Uruguay. The former two host drug production sites that have long been involved in the industry, but have, surprisingly, received scant attention. Chile and Uruguay have traditionally been seen as sites with more resilient democratic politics and higher levels of social development where drug trafficking plays only a limited role. As we shall see, however, the narco-trafficking industry has permeated and reshaped both countries' politics, economies, and state–society relations. Our examination thus seeks to complement existing work, which has focused mostly on Brazil, Mexico, Colombia (and, to a lesser extent, Central America), by concentrating on cases where criminal politics arises against the backdrop of (comparatively) lower criminal violence and (presumed) higher institutional capacity and democratic stability.

In developing this thesis, our work enters into dialogue with the flourishing literature on criminal governance. This line of study, with some exceptions (Lessing 2017; Albarracín 2018; Albarracín and Barnes 2020; Trejo and Ley 2020), has overlooked the impact criminal activities have on national politics and mainly concentrated on local politics (i.e., marginalized communities with low state presence). Going beyond existing analysis, we hypothesize that, because narco-trafficking is such a profitable industry, its weight in the overall economy is considerable (see Thoumi 2016, chapter 4) and therefore its impact on politics is significant. As some studies show, after reaching a tipping point (in terms of the illegal/legal ratio of GDP), narco-trafficking can consolidate a high-crime scenario in which associated illegal businesses expand (Bergman 2018a). Not only is the industry huge, but it seems to be growing. This seems apparent by the incidence of rising drug consumption and increased frequency of drug seizures, the multiplication and strengthening of criminal syndicates (United Nations Office on Drugs and Crime 2022, booklet 1), and by the more

---

[4] We thank Juan Albarracín for pushing us to stress this distinction and its implications for scaling up this type of research.

intangible yet critical influence that this activity is having in popular culture and in society at large (Campbell 2010; Sibila and Weiss 2014).[5]

In short, narco-trafficking has become a critical force in most Latin American countries, negatively influencing a host of politically salient issues, from security and the economy to public health and democracy. At the heart of these changes lies the incapacity of these countries' states to control, let alone eradicate, narco-trafficking, which is having several problematic effects. Recent studies have emphasized the importance of conceptualizing state capacity in relational terms, that is, measuring a state's capacity to fulfill its main functions and provide public goods (i.e., infrastructural capacity) vis-à-vis the growth and resilience of groups competing against or defying it, including organized crime (Eaton 2012; Dargent, Feldmann, and Luna 2017). According to this view, state challengers (drug traffickers in our case) accrue material and symbolic resources and easily outpace struggling states. The latter face a whole host of economic difficulties (e.g., budgetary deficits, inflationary pressures, unemployment, and growing informality), growing social demands, and acute legitimacy crises. The ramifications of the growth of state challengers are critically important because, as we will show, these challengers have altered traditional political and development dynamics.

We organize the rest of the Element as follows. Section 2 presents a brief overview of the political economy of the narcotics industry, highlighting the importance of transnational dynamics in the development of this illicit business. Subsequently, we explain how these dynamics contribute to the emergence of criminal politics and proceed to define the concept by sketching the role of criminal politics in the political economy of development. Drawing on this conceptualization, we discuss how the main protagonists of criminal politics (politicians, state agents, and criminals) interact, their incentive structure, and the outcomes of such exchanges. In Section 3 we apply our conceptual framework to our four case studies (Chile, Paraguay, Peru, and Uruguay), identifying a set of causal factors related to the most prominent manifestations of criminal politics observed in these countries. Our approach is exploratory since we do not engage in precise causal attribution at this point in the analysis. Section 4 concludes by discussing some of the relevant interactions between criminal politics and critical variables in mainstream analyses of the political economy of development. We also outline ways to better integrate the analysis of the political economy of organized crime into current accounts of development

---

[5] A chilling indicator is the growing number of citizens living in communities under the control of criminal organizations, which are often involved in this business. A recent study argues that 13 percent of the total population in Latin America – eighty million people – live under this type of arrangement (Uribe et al. 2022).

and democracy in contemporary societies. In this regard, we underscore how conventional political economy views of development are tacitly blind to how criminal politics reshapes states, politics, societal structures, and legal economic activities.

2 Conceptualizing Criminal Politics

This section describes the conditions that account for the expansion of narcotrafficking and elaborates on how the dynamics linked to this activity contribute to the emergence of our dependent variable: criminal politics. In preparing the ground for our analysis, we open the section by describing the global context driving criminal politics and then proceed to explain its main attributes.

2.1 The Context: The Political Economy of Transnational Criminal Activities

Scholars, law enforcement officials, and intelligence services have all underscored how the latest phase of globalization has had a sharp impact on contemporary criminal dynamics. The argument is straightforward: technological advances in communication, transport, and travel, coupled with the liberalization of markets, have multiplied and deepened linkages between organized crime and other actors, creating new business opportunities, a phenomenon some authors have described as deviant globalization (Gilman, Goldhammer, and Weber 2011). And although countries have reaped many benefits from globalization,[6] they have also grappled with many negative externalities,[7] including more robust and more sophisticated forms of transnational crime (Albanese 2011; Varese 2017).

The growth of sophisticated drug-trafficking organizations (DTOs) seems to be a salient feature of our globalized world (Shelley 2005; Natarajan 2019).[8] In a recent report, the UN Office on Drugs and Crime (UNODC) attributes the influence of the narcotics industry to a combination of population growth, urbanization, and a rise in general income, which has increased drug consumption worldwide (United Nations Office on Drugs and Crime 2022). Huge dividends have been derived by DTOs from a more open and interconnected world characterized by rising standards of living and the spread of consumerist

---

[6] For an overview of the development of organized crime and its links with the global economy, see Castells (2000, 169–211).

[7] Recent work has underscored the deacceleration (even reversal) of this trend in what some authors call reverse globalization; see (Crouch 2018). Even if this were the case, manifold, negative externalities of the drug industry keep emerging.

[8] These organizations have high levels of complexity characterized by a clearly defined command-and-control structure dedicated to producing, smuggling, and distributing significant quantities of illegal drugs (see Natarajan, Zanella, and Yu 2015).

patterns (Albanese 2011). This process has accelerated due to DTOs' constant experimentation and development of new products that combine controlled (pharmaceutical) and noncontrolled substances to meet rising demand (United Nations Office on Drugs and Crime 2020). A new generation of more flexible, adroit organized criminal groups has developed more up-to-date networks and taken over from older, more nationally oriented criminal mafias (Bright and Delaney 2013).

The growing power and influence of DTOs results from the unique nature of the narcotics industry, in particular its spectacular margins and the ease with which its products can be commercialized due to low obstructability (i.e., there are very few limits to the methods that can be used to traffic drugs, as criminals' limitless ingenuity attests). For their part, states have confronted significant challenges while trying to regulate and monitor growing trade volumes and human movement (Williams 2001; Andreas 1998). This has enabled DTOs to take advantage of a more porous, interconnected world and breach national boundaries by exploiting loopholes stemming from diverse administrative, political, and legal systems.[9]

While the origins and development of the international illicit narcotics industry go back several centuries (Andreas 2019; Gootenberg 2003), it has reached unprecedented proportions over the last twenty years (United Nations Office on Drugs and Crime 2020). Although the clandestine nature of the business makes it difficult to accurately determine its scale, existing studies reveal the drug-trafficking industry's staggering size. The annual retail value of the global illicit market in drugs was estimated to be US$322 billion worldwide in 2003 (United Nations Office on Drugs and Crime 2011, 31). A more recent report indicates that it is in the range of US$426 billion–US$652 billion per year and the second most profitable illicit industry behind counterfeiting and piracy (May 2017, 3). In 2018, an estimated 269 million people had consumed drugs in the previous year (5.4 percent of the world population) (United Nations Office on Drugs and Crime 2021, booklet 2, 10).[10]

---

[9] For a critical view, which argues that the role of transnational crime has been overblown, see Reuter and Tonry (2020).

[10] While displaying significant fluctuation, global drug production has shown a steady upward trend in accordance with growing demand. Opium cultivation grew from approximately 4,000 tons in 1998 to 10,270 tons in 2017; in 2018 and 2019, production dropped to 7,600 tons (United Nations Office on Drugs and Crime 2021, booklet 3, 10). Coca-bush cultivation and cocaine production show a similar trend: the former rose from 184,000 hectares in 1998 to 241,000 in 2018, while production of cocaine hydrochloride (100 percent purity) increased from 1,381 hectares in 2005 to 1,723 in 2018 (United Nations Office on Drugs and Crime 2021, booklet 3, 23). Authorities' seizure of illegal substances, generally seen as a reasonable indicator for measuring drug production, shows a marked upward trajectory. Cocaine seizures at different purity levels (e.g., cocaine hydrochloride, coca paste, and base and "crack" cocaine) reached

As we will argue, the growth of the business and the concomitant advance of DTOs has prompted a host of effects across societies, including rising violence, weakening institutions due to corruption, and erosion of state legitimacy. No country seems immune, as even the most prosperous and powerful societies, such as the Netherlands and Sweden, grapple with the challenges of drug trafficking (Holligan 2019). However, its harmful impacts have been particularly formidable in developing countries characterized by weak institutions, poor governance, and struggling economies, and where states struggle to meet the population's basic needs In these contexts, illicit activities are often the only means of surviving or attaining social mobility (Inkster and Comolli 2012). Moreover, the scale and influence of the drug industry tend to be greater in less-developed nations, where it accounts for a sizable – if unknown – percentage of national GDP (more on this in Section 2.3) (Thoumi 2003; United Nations Office on Drugs and Crime 2011). Societies experiencing conflict and war seem especially vulnerable as the business flourishes in contexts of the breakdown of the rule of law (Mantilla and Feldmann 2021) and the rise of alternative political orders (Arjona, Kasfir, and Mampilly 2015), which often end up creating major security challenges (Kan 2016).

Latin America, in particular, has had to cope with a remarkably vigorous drug industry (Clawson and Lee 1996; Gootenberg 2008). Here, the industry has prospered against the backdrop of struggling economies characterized by structural weaknesses, including an overreliance on commodities, macroeconomic imbalances, and a large informal sector. Notwithstanding significant variation, illicit narcotics have brought criminal activities, violence, and corruption to every country in the region, irrespective of preexisting levels of state capacity and innovative frameworks for coping with emerging criminal dynamics like marijuana legalization and ambitious police and judicial reforms (Bergman 2018b, 60–68).

Two other economic trends have reinforced the transformational influence of drug trafficking in Latin America: the commodity boom (2005–15) prompted by rising demand for raw materials produced in the region and the gig economy. Together, these forces have critically reshaped the political economy of development, transforming the scope and nature of the region's extensive informal economies. For instance, the drug industry has expanded by exploiting synergies with the gig economy by developing new app-mediated micro-trafficking and money-laundering practices (Davis and Hilgers 2022).[11] The expansion of

---

1,311 tons in 2018, and 55 percent of seizures occurred in Latin America. With respect to opium-derived products, authorities seized 704 tons of opium, 97 tons of heroin, and 42 tons of morphine in 2018 (United Nations Office on Drugs and Crime 2021, booklet 3, 12.21–23).

[11] Our sources have stressed the significance of this emerging trend.

mining and intensive agriculture also provided opportunities for narco-trafficking, especially by expanding countries' import and export activities. While imports bring in chemicals used in drug manufacturing, export activities widen options for smuggling drugs to different international destinations. As with other commodities (agricultural and mining products), the drug economy has produced significant (and politically consequential) externalities for countries' institutions and societies. The drug economy also creates regulatory challenges for relatively weak state bureaucracies which struggle to police highly disruptive and rapidly changing market innovations. An expanding economy also provides further opportunities for money laundering. More worrisome still, at a time when the formal economy's growth has slowed, and the catastrophic socioeconomic effects of the COVID-19 pandemic and the impact of the Russian military invasion of Ukraine are starting to become more apparent, the drug economy is providing (countercyclical) opportunities for economic growth and consumption.

Against the backdrop of struggling states seemingly unable to address massive social problems, criminal syndicates, often perceived as more effective and responsive than authorities, augment their strength and legitimacy in under-served communities (Muggah and Dudley 2021; Davis and Hilgers 2022). Drug-trafficking influence goes far beyond marginal communities, however. It is also embedded in vertically and horizontally integrated activities and commodity chains, with various linkages across other industries, some legal and some not. These pervasive dynamics remain obscured in the literature.

The International Drug Control Regime (IDCR) constitutes another essential contextual factor influencing drug-trafficking dynamics. Enshrined in a series of international treaties and conventions,[12] the IDCR consists of norms and regulations seeking to curb the production, commercialization, and consumption of psychoactive substances (Nadelmann 1990; Andreas and Nadelmann 2008; Idler 2021). The IDCR, whose normative rejection of drug consumption is informed by religious (puritan) views (Courtwright 2019), has had a profound impact on the general understanding and perception of this problem and has pushed the industry into illegality (Gootenberg 2021). Concomitantly, it has constrained countries' range of drug control policies. As a result, most efforts have been directed at stemming the supply side and thus have disproportionally targeted drug-producing and drug-transit countries (Inkster and Comolli 2012). This regime is reinforced by a powerful intergovernmental bureaucracy (comprising Interpol and UN machinery, including agencies and treaty oversight

---

[12] The IDCR's three most important treaties include: the Single Convention of Narcotic Drugs (1961), amended by the 1972 Protocol; the Convention on Psychotropic Substances (1971); and the Convention against Illicit Traffic in Narcotic Drugs and Psychotropic Substances (1988).

mechanisms) charged with combating different facets of the drug business, which often opposes reforms to legalize the industry (McAllister 2012). Despite its fragmented nature and problematic approach,[13] the regime plays a large role in shaping the nature and logic of the illicit drug industry (Hallam and Bewley-Taylor 2021).

Since World War II, the United States has become the most consequential – and fervent –supporter of the IDCR (Nadelmann 1990; Gootenberg 2008). While Washington has pursued its war on drugs on a global scale, its efforts have concentrated on Latin America, in particular cocaine production (Benítez 2014; Andreas 2019). Since the Reagan administration, drug policy has been at the top of the bilateral agenda between the United States and Latin America (Schoultz 1999; Chabat 2012; Rosen 2014). The United States has imposed its particular view of the drugs trade by combining a law enforcement, zero-tolerance approach that criminalizes commercialization and consumption domestically (Nadelmann 1990; Levine 2003; Andreas and Nadelmann 2008) with aggressive international measures to curb the production and transshipment of drugs into its territory by distributing military aid (training, assistance, equipment) and counter-narcotics assistance to major producer countries (Loweman 2006). Several agencies, most prominently the Department of Defense, the State Department and law enforcement agencies such as the Drug Enforcement Agency (DEA), have been at the forefront of international efforts to combat the illicit narcotics industry in source countries (Bewley-Taylor 2012; Andreas 2019).

In sum, there seems to be a widespread consensus that narco-trafficking represents a significant challenge and that it has not been met with effective policies, either at domestic or international arenas in Latin America and beyond (Durán-Martínez 2021). That societies are grappling with this issue is reflected in a recent open manifesto by a group of former Latin American presidents, who unequivocally state: "Violence and the organized crime associated with the narcotics trade are critical problems in Latin America today. Confronted with a situation that is growing worse by the day, it is imperative to rectify the 'war on drugs' strategy pursued in the region over the past 30 years" (Latin American Commission on Drugs and Democracy 2020, 7).

2.2 Conceptualizing Criminal Politics

> I am alone and must operate alone. If I pick up the phone and talk to the police, I also speak to the narcos, the senators, and the justice system. They are all the same, and they work together.[14]

---

[13] For a critical view of the regime, see Idler (2021).

[14] Personal conversation with an antidrug attorney, funded by the DEA, in Asunción, 2013.

The expansion and growing influence attained by drug trafficking in Latin America are altering in meaningful ways how politics operate in every country. The resources and influence this multimillion-dollar business generates have impacted the incentive structure of incumbent politicians who, instead of combating this illicit activity, adopt a pragmatic stance toward the business, harnessing the benefits it brings while seeking to minimize some of its many problematic aspects. In the words of a top Uruguayan official in the government of the Frente Amplio (Broad Front, 2005–20): "If drug trafficking injects much money into the economy of underserved communities without generating visible costs [i.e., violence, corruption scandals], politicians can look the other way and benefit, directly and indirectly, from the expanding business."[15] Beyond obtaining material means for resource-starved communities, politicians may also benefit from the help of criminal organizations in the discharge of their duties, including the provision of order and surrogate social assistance to areas the state is not willing or able to govern effectively. Monies originating in the drug market also create spillovers into consumption, public works, and private investment. In other words, while politicians and state agents are often portrayed as antagonistic to drug traffickers, they may seek mutually beneficial arrangements (Lupsha 1983; Lessing 2021).[16] Revenues from the drugs industry also inject critical resources into the legal economy (see Thoumi 2016).

While the interaction between illicit industries, politicians, and the legal economy has historical antecedents in several countries in the region (e.g., Mexico, Paraguay, and Colombia) (Camacho 2006; Snyder and Durán-Martínez 2009), the depth of these links seems to be growing and extending to more countries, as some of our case studies highlight. To the extent that many politicians and state agents' careers have become entangled with this illicit activity, either because they are compromised and use the activity as a way to further their own goals (economic, political, personal), fear for their security, or are constrained in their capacity to act because they lack the resources to confront narco-trafficking, the nature of how they exercise power and behave politically has changed. In this respect, Bergman (2018b) posits that Latin America is approaching the tipping point that separates low-crime equilibriums (i.e., those that characterize developed societies and, until recently, several countries in the region) from high-crime equilibriums. As we will also argue, the latter consolidate via multiple mechanisms through which criminal activities reshape politics, institutions, society, and the economy.

---

[15] Personal conversation, Montevideo, 2021.
[16] These authors describe the nature of the relationship as symbiotic.

The real impact of the drugs industry on politics is difficult to ascertain because, as Arias (2017) reminds us, the nature of the phenomenon is fuzzy and, therefore, hard to conceptualize (see also Trejo and Ley 2020, 39). The opaque nature of the links between these actors, the shifting rules informing the interaction among participants, and the fluidity and multiple categories of actors involved (e.g., legal, illegal, local, supralocal, etc.) render even an accurate description of them exceedingly challenging. Recent work, particularly the emerging literature on criminal governance, has contributed a series of insights concerning the role the narcotics industry plays on politically relevant dimensions, including its effects on societal violence (Durán-Martínez 2018; Yashar 2018), the functioning of the state (Koonings 2012), and governance (Auyero 2007; Moncada 2016; Albarracín 2018; Lessing 2021).[17] Another essential contribution is Barnes' work linking criminal organizations and the production of violence more explicitly to politico-institutional factors (Barnes 2017).[18]

While this literature is commendable for its accurate description and strong conceptualization of the organized crime–state nexus, it is only beginning to shed light on how criminality affects politics. Part of the problem is that it focuses primarily on local politics.[19] To add to these difficulties, the nature of criminal politics shifts significantly across time and space. In the temporal domain, exogenous shocks (e.g., market or technological disruptions, political turnover, geopolitical influence, etc.) can readily disrupt criminal politics at a given moment. In the spatial domain, different local configurations can be observed within the same country – across formal jurisdictions, across segments of several formal jurisdictions, or only in specific spaces within jurisdictions (see Snyder and Durán-Martínez 2009). In this regard, the specific configuration of criminal politics in terms of its overlap with formal jurisdictions is crucial to grasping this phenomenon, as it determines the patterns of integration/rivalry between criminal organizations, state agents, and politicians.

In his influential "brown areas" paper, O'Donnell (1993) conceives the political topography of Latin American states as a mosaic of brown, green,

---

[17] For an overview of this literature, see Mantilla and Feldmann (2021) and Albarracín and Barnes (2020).

[18] Barnes (2017, 973) conceptualizes criminal politics as links "between states and violent organizations that are motivated more by the accumulation of wealth and informal power, and which seldom have formal political ambitions pertaining to the state itself."

[19] Extant work displays some theoretical blind spots and methodological biases and does not systematically discuss how illicit industries and organized crime affect institutions, relevant socio-political phenomena, and economic development. By primarily focusing on the most sensational manifestations of drug trafficking in contemporary societies (violence and corruption, often at the local and neighborhood levels), the available research on organized crime and drug trafficking rarely explores the broader implications of such economic activity in reshaping legal economies and state and political institutions (see Feldmann and Luna 2022).

and blue areas representing different state–society configurations. Building on O'Donnell's seminal insight, we posit that criminal politics schemes vary significantly depending on how state agents, politicians, and narco-trafficking organizations relate across different territorial (i.e., communities) and functional (i.e., customs, logistics, finance) arenas. Observed differences also arise according to the relative importance and social visibility that different phases of the narco-trafficking business (i.e., production, micro-trafficking, macro-trafficking, money laundering) have in each country. In other words, relevant *places* for criminal politics arise either in territorial or functional arenas, depending on each country's configuration of the criminal side of criminal politics.[20] For example, seaports, border areas, financial systems, real estate, and legal businesses are critical in countries where macro-trafficking and money-laundering activities predominate. These arenas are not territorial but functional. In addition, they are often less conspicuous and visible to the public. Micro-trafficking and drug production are often thought to require territorial control by DTOs and tend to be more socially visible.[21]

Another critical aspect concerns how illegal activities (i.e., different phases of narco-trafficking) and legal activities are vertically (i.e., from the local to the national level) and horizontally (i.e., across criminal and legal economic activities) integrated. The available research often deals with cases where there exists a modicum of cartelization (which produces vertical and horizontal integration). However, the cases we analyze in this Element suggest that cartelization is not necessary for observing massive criminal politics. Thus, the scope of possible combinations observed within countries in the configuration of narco-trafficking activities implies that variations across time and space concerning different criminal activities do not necessarily aggregate in an orderly manner, either territorially or functionally.

In short, our work seeks to complement existing research on criminal governance by scaling up the analysis and interrogating how the criminal organizations participating in the drug-trafficking industry impact high politics, state institutions, and, concomitantly, development. Rather than taking issue with existing work in the field, our analytical framework seeks to buttress extant knowledge by refining the definition of criminal politics, elaborating theoretically on its logic and attributes, and attempting to explore it empirically.

---

[20] We use *place* in reference to spaces as a combination of geography, location, practices, logic, and meaningfulness where rules and norms are collectively constructed (see Gieryn 2000).

[21] Recently, drug production and micro-trafficking have become increasingly nonterritorial due to the introduction of new chemical drugs and the irruption of app-mediated micro-trafficking transactions (personal interviews in Chile and Uruguay during 2020–2).

2.3 Criminal Politics and the Political Economy of Development

The traditional literature on the political economy of development analyzes interactions among business, politicians, and state institutions. According to the conventional wisdom, these exchanges happen against the backdrop of international dynamics linked to the economy, which, along with geopolitical factors, influence domestic outcomes. These exchanges compose the legal political economy of development (hereafter, we refer to this as L). In contexts where criminal politics is pervasive (e.g., Afghanistan, Burma, Paraguay), if the economy were depicted as an iceberg, L would represent the tip of the iceberg. Beneath the surface lies an illegal political economy (hereafter, we refer to this as I) constituted by the exchanges and interactions among organized crime actors, politicians, and state institutions. Moreover, both political economies (L and I) have a porous interface, which we claim is the locus of criminal politics. Within this space, which Auyero (2007) in his seminal work terms a "grey zone," actors from both political economies often interact.[22] Figure 1 graphically illustrates the nature of L, I, and their interface (criminal politics).

The "iceberg" that depicts criminal politics' locus in countries' political economy is not the prototypical one in which the hidden part is often much more significant than its visible tip. In most countries, L is

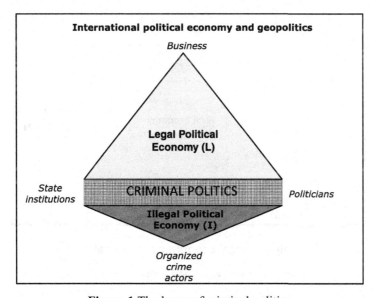

Figure 1 The locus of criminal politics

Source: Authors' construction.

---

[22] The Mexican poet Javier Sicilia metaphorically describes it as *the mud* (see Sicilia 2016).

significantly more extensive and relevant in accounting for the country's GDP than I.[23] The relative size of I varies across contexts in fundamental ways. It is much more prominent in underdeveloped nations. In his work on Colombia, one of the few systematically investigated cases, Francisco Thoumi calculated that the drug industry accounted for 7 percent of the country's GDP in the 1980s and 3–4 percent in the 1990s (Thoumi 2016, 112), while a recent study placed it at 3 percent between 2015–18 (Montenegro, LLano, and Ibañez 2019). The Inter-American Drug Abuse Control Commission (2013) estimated that retail sales exclusively amounted to US$320 billion, or 0.9 percent of GDP at the regional level in 2012 (see also Holmes and de Piñeres 2006). We posit that criminal politics, even if still not dominant in absolute terms, becomes highly consequential for development when the I/L ratio hits a theoretical threshold – or a tipping point in Bergman's terminology. Figure 2 illustrates three ideal-typical settings by comparing countries' economies in

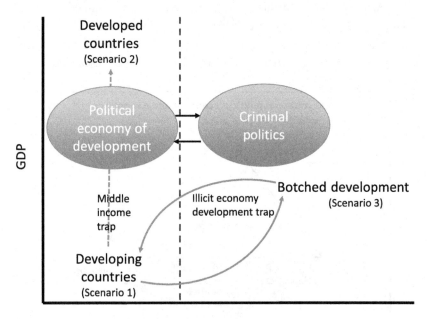

Figure 2 Criminal politics and illicit economy development traps

Source: Authors' construction.

---

[23] The UNODC reports that flows linked to this industry and associated with transnational criminal organizations accounted for US$650 billion or 1.5 percent of global GDP in 2009 (United Nations Office on Drugs and Crime 2011).

terms of the relative size of L, I, and their countries' GDP. While criminality and politics interact in all countries, in developed ones, where the magnitude of illegal business represents a small proportion of the economy, the extension of criminal politics is more restrictive. Conversely, in developing nations, where the weight of illicit industries is relatively greater, the role of criminal politics rises and becomes crucial in understanding development trajectories.

Developing countries with smaller, less dynamic legal political economies often need help to provide public services, generate employment, and produce essential goods for the population. In such scenarios, illicit activities often offer a critical lifeline that keeps the economy afloat and provides people with badly needed economic opportunities. However, the influx of illegal resources, which technically could raise the population's standard of living, comes at the price of extensive corruption and state capture. This negatively impacts the nature and quality of politics and institutions, thus undermining development.

Classic and contemporary works on the political economy of development emphasize the nature of state and political institutions as critical levers explaining development and underdevelopment (Acemoglu, Johnson, and Robinson 2005; Donner and Schneider 2016; Acemoglu and Robinson 2019). Most of these accounts invoke long-term, usually path-dependent explanations of institutional quality (Mahoney 2010; Mazzuca and Munck 2021). The causal role of criminal politics in shaping developmental trajectories is different. Although long-term institutional quality deficits predispose countries to criminal politics, the latter's expansion is also critically shaped by criminal dynamics capable of offsetting long-term endowments and positive developments in the realm of institutional and state building as Dargent, Feldmann, and Luna (2017) show in the Peruvian case. Chile and Uruguay, both of which are often considered high-capacity states with good quality democratic institutions – at least in the Latin American context – today confront significant challenges, which can, at least in part, be attributed to the expansion of criminal politics. Such an increase is likely to reduce their long-term institutional quality endowments intertemporally.

The spread of criminal politics thus critically reshapes countries' development trajectories, a dynamic depicted in Figure 2. Scenario 1, in that figure, depicts underdeveloped economies, while scenario 2 depicts developed ones. The conventional wisdom, captured by the classical literature, conceptualizes development as the transition from scenario 1 to scenario 2. The political economy of such a transition is usually analyzed in terms of the configurations of natural endowments, institutional features, and productive innovations, which render the transition to a higher developmental stage possible. Failed transitions are often explained by identifying development traps, such as the middle-income trap (see Donner and Schneider 2016). Scenario 3 depicts the role of criminal politics in generating a different type of development trap, one we shall call a "botched development trap." In that scenario, the relative expansion of the illegal economy makes criminal politics more and more consequential for the legal political economy and its institutions and generates negative externalities (corruption, violence, institutional decay). As Figure 2 indicates, countries can eventually increase their GDP under such a scenario. For instance, Paraguay and Peru grew steadily at a time when the production of both legal and illegal economies expanded significantly. Nevertheless, their development is problematic and has been accompanied by the spread of corruption, institutional erosion, and rising violence in some locations (Amambay in Paraguay, La Libertad in Peru). In Section 2.4, we will also claim that botched development reinforces development traps through its impact over time on political and state institutions.

Although a precise estimation of the I/L threshold triggering a transition from scenario 2 to scenario 3 is virtually impossible to obtain (and might vary contextually across societies), its implications are empirically traceable. Illegal economies do not need to be omnipresent in society to limit state capacity while imposing significant constraints on politicians. In this regard, we favor a relational approach to state capacity (Migdal 2001; Eaton 2012; Dargent, Feldmann and Luna 2017). According to this view, state challengers (drug traffickers in our case) can accrue sufficient material and symbolic resources to outcompete efforts by politicians and public bureaucracies to build state capacity, exploiting local asymmetries between the parties involved.[24] Moreover, while states move slowly, are territorially bounded, and may confront stringent budgetary and redistributive constraints, criminal organizations are not territorially bounded, can relocate quickly, and have access to massive resources. These dynamics hurt development prospects (Paredes and Manrique 2021).

In sum, when criminal organizations produce enough resources to infiltrate parts of the state, they often begin reshaping legal business activities and capturing state institutions and the political system (instead of being contained by the legal political economy of a country). In such a scenario, the implication is that the threshold or tipping point described by Bergman (2018b) has been hit.

---

[24] For instance, (Dewey 2016) and Auyero and Sobering (2019) provide ample evidence of how in Argentina, the police and politicians hold the upper hand and selectively deploy enforcement in certain areas in accordance with their interests. (Smilde, Zubillaga, and Hanson 2022) show a similar pattern in Venezuela, where a repressive state holds some sway over gangs. Conversely, the most important Mexican DTOs have enough power to extricate themselves from the control of central states and thus demonstrate significantly more capacity to shape the nature of politics, notwithstanding intrusion by state agents (Trejo and Ley 2020).

We contend that, in recent years, the expansion of the drug market has created a transition from scenario 2 to scenario 3, even in unusual suspects such as Chile and Uruguay. Such a transition has important implications for how we think about development and institutions, which we will begin to unpack in the remainder of this Element.

2.4 Actors, Incentives, and Exchanges

In this section we describe the interactive dynamic informing the exchange among criminal politics' three main actors (politicians, state agents, and drug traffickers). Figure 3 illustrates our discussion.

As shown in Figure 3, drug traffickers furnish resources to politicians through bribes and also indirectly by helping to establish order, create jobs, and spur economic dynamism in localities under their control. Drug traffickers can also produce negative rents for politicians by increasing violence and spreading corruption. They can also violently shape political competition in favor of allied politicians by using targeted violence against their rivals and foes (Albarracín 2018). Politicians, for their part, have leverage over criminal groups because if they decide to enforce the rule of law in localities and functional arenas where criminals operate, they can disrupt their businesses. Principal–agent dilemmas arise when state agents, who can be bribed by criminals and who can act autonomously, enforce politicians' decisions. In other words, in settings where criminal politics is pervasive, drug traffickers can challenge state actors and politicians and offer much-needed order and

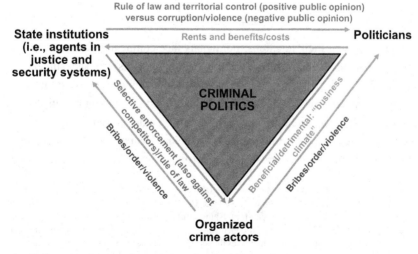

Figure 3 Main actors and exchanges shaping criminal politics
Source: Authors' construction.

financial resources to the communities they control, which politicians and citizens support (Arias 2017; Lessing 2021). This type of scenario presents important dilemmas for political action. Constrained by scarce resources and supported by weak, patrimonial, and often unaccountable state bureaucracies, Latin American politicians need to decide whether to allocate resources – and how much – to enforce their (otherwise tacit) monopoly of coercion and how to distribute those resources across localities and functional arenas.

In a prototypical example, local territorial orders and functional arenas are heterogeneous with regard to the varying presence of interactions observed between politicians, state agents, and criminal organizations. At any given time, states can only deploy limited resources to defend their coercive monopoly from challengers (Eaton 2012). In other words, the configuration of criminal politics depends on the interaction between criminal structures linked to organized crime and countries' unique politico-institutional dynamics. The latter result from (i) politicians' will and/or (ii) the behavior of state agents, who may leverage principal–agent dilemmas in their (possibly deviant) implementation of political decisions and public policies. Within this framework, we can develop expectations about actors' behavior and incentives from recent insights concerning contingent political decisions to suspend the enforcement of the rule of law when engaging certain groups and localities (Slater and Kim 2015; Dewey 2016; Holland 2017). We start by analyzing the incentives faced by politicians and state agents. The actions of both types of actors constitute the *political* side of criminal politics. We subsequently turn to analyze the *criminal* side and its possible determinants.[25]

2.4.1 Politicians

While exercising their functions, politicians face competing demands for the provision of public goods (security, infrastructure, services) from constituencies upon whom their political fortunes depend. Politicians need to weigh how to balance simultaneous demands on the part of the different communities they serve against other state functions (e.g., deterring external threats, developing an effective central state bureaucracy).[26] Beyond scarce resource allocation, enforcing public policy across localities and functional arenas with DTO

---

[25] We are mindful that politicians' and state agents' ideal types of response are not independent of criminal activity and that both are coconstituted. For the sake of clarity, however, we examine them separately. We thank Ines Fynn for pushing us to clarify this.

[26] Such decisions are likely to be path-dependent (i.e., the presence of state infrastructure and personnel in one locality at time t increases the likelihood of observing subsequent allocations at times $t+n$). However, we assume that at any stage, politicians might also decide to pull resources out of areas in which further investments are seen as redundant, non-productive, or only marginally useful.

influence represents a particularly thorny task for politicians mindful that state enforcers may be exposed to violence and corruption.

We assume the political decision to deploy the state's coercive monopoly is a function of two basic parameters that are relatively invariant over time. One parameter is the availability of resources in the local economy that can be tapped for political use. The other is the size of the local population, which renders the location electorally more or less relevant for politicians. Regarding the latter point, we hypothesize that densely populated and resource-rich areas have greater leverage over politicians DTOs and therefore tend to be more salient in their eyes. Three additional conditions impact politicians' calculations. First, politicians are often risk averse and may decide not to deploy resources to reclaim a location if doing so could trigger conflicts with local groups or risk escalating a conflict that might subsequently threaten their rule in other areas of the country (Boone 2012). Second, the salience of a given location might eventually grow as a function of increased public attention, irrespective of a relatively fixed population and potential rents. For instance, spiraling violence or corruption scandals in an area might raise its salience in politicians' eyes, especially if media and influential interests raise the issue in society (Saín 2002). Against this backdrop, politicians might shift enforcement allocations from one place to another. And third, politicians might – and often do – seek to extract rents from criminals via the conditional enforcement of the rule of law. To credibly commit to conditional nonenforcement in exchange for rents, politicians ought to be able to enforce the law (Dewey, Miguez, and Saín 2017).

Political actors confronting a surge in criminal activity face a trilemma or 'unholy trinity' (Lessing 2017): how to combat criminality, stem corruption, and decrease violence at the same time. According to Lessing, it is simply impossible to address these three ills simultaneously: at most, only two of these objectives can be pursued at once.[27] This trilemma plays out differently across jurisdictions. Politicians face distributive incentives that shape their behavior in terms of whether to tolerate spirals of violence in specific local contexts (Holland 2017), which are likely driven by the relative electoral costs and gains associated with suspending law enforcement in specific territorial and socioeconomic enclaves (Dewey 2012; Zarazaga 2014).

Politicians, however, also see potential benefits while dealing with drug-related activities. As indicated, the resources provided by this illicit business can boost investment and consumption in the legal economy. Surrogate

---

[27] The logic is as follows: increasing repressive power to deter DTOs inadvertently gives enforcers more power, thus creating incentives for corruption. The reverse is also true: implementing anti-corruption measures might push DTOs to engage in violence to counter the rising costs of bribery (Lessing 2017, 291).

governance schemes may also be provided by DTOs in places where politicians decide not to invest state resources (Arias 2006; Barnes 2017). For example, suppose criminal organizations contribute to producing economic and welfare spillovers and much-needed funding for party/electoral activities without generating violence, either in a locality or a functional arena. In that case, politicians have a short-term incentive to protect criminals and profit from illegal activities. However, corruption may become politicized and create electoral costs so that those same politicians eventually have an incentive to combat criminal activities (Lessing 2017).[28] In other words, politicians confront a trade-off between positive and negative externalities associated with drug-trafficking activities. If the political costs of drug trafficking are high (i.e., if violence, corruption, or both gain traction in public opinion), they have incentives to take publicly visible action against crime. This is consistent with a contestation scenario. But suppose, instead, the drug economy benefits incumbents (either personally through bribes or at the aggregate level through economic spillovers from the drug economy) without creating public controversy. In that case, politicians are incentivized to engage in collusive arrangements with DTOs. This is consistent with a rent-seeking scenario. Eventually, politicians could "look the other way" and unilaterally forbear enforcement under a nonengagement scenario.

Hence, with regard to politicians' responses to organized crime, we distinguish three scenarios. Politicians can either *contest* organized crime presence, *seek rents* from criminals, or *forbear* (look away and decide not to engage criminals) in a specific place/function. Although empirically adjudicating between these three scenarios when applied to specific real-world instances is very difficult, it is critical for conceptual clarity. In low-salience places, we expect politicians either not to engage with criminals or to seek to extract rent from them (contestation is less frequent in this type of setting). Criminal syndicates specializing in activities requiring some territorial control have a greater need to require tacit or explicit allegiance from local populations and are more likely to engage with local politicians. Those involved in activities which engage functional areas of the state that lack a fixed territory and population do not often attract public attention, even if they might often produce sizable rents that are attractive for politicians and state agents.

Conversely, when criminal activities arise in places characterized by greater salience, politicians might seek to tighten enforcement by adopting "strong

---

[28] In their insightful work, Trejo and Ley (2017, 2020) show how Mexican politicians may deploy coercion selectively to reward loyalists and punish detractors and the opposition.

hand," "zero tolerance," and "war on drugs" policies. Strict enforcement leads to contestation between criminal organizations and politicians. Contestation often escalates violence at the local level, where DTOs defend their turf. In less salient activities, contestation often leads to political scandals involving prominent national figures. Our opening vignette in Section 1 is a case in point, as factional and partisan turf wars like the one observed between Colorado Party factions in Paraguay led to contestation at this level.

Based on this reasoning, we assume that politicians' behavior is contingent on the trade-off between the benefits and costs of drug trafficking. The visibility of drug trafficking to the public, especially the visibility of violence, corruption, or both, drives politicians' to prioritize costs over benefits. Naturally, however, politicians face additional constraints. For instance, the international prohib-ition regime pushes for enforcement (often against the will of local politicians) and raises the social visibility of drug trafficking. Institutional incentives and the formal prerogatives of different political actors (e.g., mayors, municipal council members, congressional members, regional governors, national polit-ical parties, etc.) are also critical in determining politicians' engagement with criminals. In specific institutional contexts, for example, local (municipal) authorities regulate pivotal arenas that impact organized crime activities, while on other occasions regulation and enforcement hinge upon national or regional authorities.

Finally, drug-trafficking activities differ in terms of their visibility. Micro-trafficking in urban peripheries can readily become more socially visible. However, activities such as production in rural areas or international smuggling and money laundering are generally the least visible, even if their economic rents are often much more substantial. For this reason, it is empirically relevant to analyze how different drug trafficking activities and their relative visibility guide politicians' cost–benefit calculations.[29]

2.4.2 State Agents

The ways in which politicians engage with organized crime are not only influenced by the strategies they have at their disposal while interacting with criminal groups. They often also depend on state agents. However, it is critical to assume that politicians and state agents do not always act in concert. As a result, criminal politics also gets configured through the principal–agent dilemmas whereby state agents may subvert politicians'

---

[29] Additional complications could be introduced by considering different types of politicians (i.e., local vs. national ones; opposition vs. incumbent politicians).

will for their own gain. In other words, the implementation of political decisions is contingent, to a significant degree, on enforcement by state agents such as police and judicial actors. According to our fieldwork, and consistent with extant theory (Ross 1973; Jensen and Meckling 1976), two factors drive state agents' behavior on the ground: institutional fragmentation and the (functional) autonomy of state agents from their principals (elected politicians). Where institutional fragmentation triggers competition among law enforcement and judicial system actors, many opportunities arise for criminal organizations to selectively corrupt and co-opt state agents and institutions. In institutionally atomized systems, the relative endowments of different law enforcement agencies are also pivotal. The specialized literature has offered ample evidence of this dynamic, especially in the case of Mexico (Trejo and Ley 2017; Durán-Martínez 2018).

The relative autonomy of state agents from their formal principals also shapes enforcement in any given place. Principal–agent dilemmas can work either way and bend political will toward illegality or enforcement. However, in extreme cases like that of the Buenos Aires Provincial Police, the principal–agent relationship is in reverse because police forces are the principal architects of "clandestine orders" within their districts (Auyero 2007; Dewey 2016). In such a context, police departments fund political campaigns with resources obtained through systematic bribes and are thus able to set conditions for political competition at local and sometimes provincial levels (Flom 2022). The police, in coordination with criminal organizations, can also provoke a public security crisis in localities where the political authorities do not comply with their (tacit) rule (see Saín 2002).

Three-way, complex interactions among politicians, state agents, and organized crime are also frequent.[30] Again, in the case of Argentina, Dewey (2016) documents empirically how cooperative interactions with organized crime allow state agents not only to extract economic resources for their benefit, and to finance political campaigns in their district, but also to fund essential state operations (e.g., buying office supplies for police stations) for which the state budget falls short.

Bribes are just one practice sustaining these complex interactions. In Brazil, harsh enforcement policies in prison systems in the 1990s (especially in the state of São Paulo) inadvertently contributed to the emergence of the Primeiro Comando da Capital (PCC), a powerful prison gang (see Biondi 2016;

---

[30] There is a broad spectrum of collaboration, from mild forms, including "looking the other way," to robust forms of cooperation, including fully fledged alliances; see Arias (2017).

Feltran, 2018). Organizations like the PCC and Rio's Commando Vermelho (CV), which now dominate Brazilian jails (in theory, the epitome of state power), also control parts of many major Brazilian cities (Willis 2015; Biondi 2016; Insight Crime 2020). Criminal governance schemes are, therefore, pivotal, not only for organized crime operations but also for providing public goods such as conflict-resolution services and social assistance. Greater order in the streets also benefits politicians and state agents, whose operations are constrained by (relationally) weak state capacity (Davis and Hilgers 2022; Lessing 2022).

Building on these premises, we conceptualize the political side of criminal politics as entailing different bribing structures and targets. Table 1 introduces six ideal types that result from politicians' three possible strategies – forbear, contest, or seek rents – and the presence/absence of significant principal–agent dilemmas between politicians and state agents. If politicians seek rents and can effectively bring state agents into compliance, the former structure a *protection racket*. In cases where politicians seek rents but cannot ensure that the bureaucracy follows their orders, or if politicians lack sufficient coordination and seek rents independently, *Janus-faced corruption* ensues. In the latter case, politicians and state agents seek rents in a more atomized and decentralized fashion since politicians cannot unify rent-seeking interactions with criminals. Under contestation, state agents might deviate from their principal's mandates and get bribed as well, rendering politicians' "tough on crime" policies mere *lip service* lacking enforcement. Alternatively, if politicians decide to contest and state agents go along with their mandate, enforcement policies approach an *iron fist* ideal type. However, if politicians decide to forbear, state agents on the ground can still seek rents, thus giving rise to *opportunistic corruption*. The scenario where state agents instead comply (or

Table 1 Politicians' and state agents' responses to criminal activity

Is there a massive principal–agent problem?	Politicians' strategy		
	Forbear	**Contest**	**Rent-seek**
Yes	Opportunistic (administrative) corruption	Lip service	Janus-faced (political, administrative) corruption
No	Standoff	Iron fist	Protection racket

their actions are nonconsequential on the ground, given their scarce presence in a location) yields the *standoff* ideal type.

We will show more extensively in our case studies how diverse criminal politics arrangements generate significantly different outcomes. Each type leads to specific patterns of corruption, state capture, and externalities derived from it (e.g., violence). Situations in which politicians opt not to engage with criminal actors or privilege extracting rents from them are usually not openly violent. However, they might entail high levels of structural violence against local communities. Alternatively, contestation generally produces more violence and corruption (Lessing 2017).

2.4.3 Criminal Actors

We now turn to analyze how DTOs impact criminal politics and the logic of their operation. To provide context for our analysis, we first present a succinct contextual description of the rise of DTOs, underlining how some of their attributes (e.g., characteristics, institutional trajectory, setting, and power) shape their incentive structure. As indicated, the steady growth and influence of the drug-trafficking industry is strongly impacting Latin American societies, irrespective of their politico-institutional endowments. We posit that while transnational factors linked to the drug-trafficking industry and contributing to the emergence of powerful criminal syndicates impact all countries, domestic considerations linked to countries' specific roles in the narcotics business (i.e., competitive advantages, criminal landscapes) account for differences in their position in the industry, something that, as we will see, impacts the nature of criminal politics, too.

In her classic study of international political economy, Strange (1996) emphasizes how powerful global structural forces have significantly limited the capacity of individual states to pursue their preferred policies. Strange discusses the role of illicit industries and criminal syndicates in this process, explaining how such dynamics siphon power away from states to ever more powerful nonstate actors. The drug industry's singular nature, in particular its outsized margins, has created the conditions for the emergence of mighty DTOs which operate transnationally and can challenge modern states. Using their vast resources, these organizations strive to influence or control all facets of the business, from production to distribution and across multiple settings, to attain a dominant position. Large DTOs, primarily operating in complex networks (Bruinsma and Bernasco 2004), set the conditions for the participation of smaller less sophisticated players at the local level (Natarajan, Zanella, and Yu 2015; Von Lampe 2016).[31]

---

[31] On the relationship between transnational and local organizations, see Hobbs (1998); on the relationship between drug trafficking and mafia structures, see Calderoni (2012).

Developments in the Latin American drug-trafficking industry over the last thirty years since the boom and bust of the powerful Cali and Medellín DTOs reflect this trend. After securing a dominant position in Colombia, these organizations quickly expanded, developing a transnational multimillion-dollar operation. At the zenith of their power, the Cali and Medellín DTOs almost singlehandedly controlled the drug business across the entire Western Hemisphere and even ventured further afield to Europe and Asia. Smaller criminal syndicates were subservient, operating under the terms dictated by Cali and Medellín, primarily as providers and intermediaries (Duncan 2015b). The vacuum left by their demise at the hands of a Colombian–American alliance in the 1990s was filled by the meteoric rise of several Mexican DTOs (e.g., Sinaloa, Gulf, Juárez, Arellano-Felix-Cartel).[32] These groups evolved from being intermediaries for the Colombian DTOs – moving drugs across the US border – to being the chief protagonists of the business (Shirk and Wallman 2015; Esberg 2020; UC San Diego 2021).

Today, the power and influence of Mexican DTOs extends far beyond Mexico, reaching most of the Western Hemisphere and even other regions (Grillo 2015). The ever-growing Brazilian DTOs, including the CV and especially the PCC, alongside Colombian and Mexican organizations, constitute the third critical player in the region. Due to their spectacular rise, PCC and CV have not only become the dominant forces in Brazil's large market, but have extended their influence into neighboring countries (Carvalho and Soares 2016; Feltran 2018; Insight Crime 2020).

Several prosecutors and law enforcement agents interviewed for this study emphasize how, over the years, Mexican, Brazilian, and Colombian DTOs have built sophisticated operations. These groups have leveraged their vast resources and expertise to vertically integrate different phases of the business (i.e., production, trafficking, money laundering) and consolidate their dominant position.[33] Smaller local criminal organizations usually work as their subcontractors, intermediaries, and providers, often moving drugs and concentrating on alternative, less profitable markets such as cocaine base paste and marijuana (Insight Crime 2021a). As a result, DTOs with the capacity to operate transnationally act as gatekeepers, using their power to prevent the rise of competing

---

[32] Colombian DTOs have weakened because of the fragmentation of the market following the demise of Medellín and Cali, and been replaced by groups including the Gaitanista Self-Defense of Colombia and guerrillas that have become involved in the drug business, such as the National Liberation Army (ELN) and dissident splinter groups from the now-dissolved Revolutionary Armed Forces of Colombia (FARC) (Feldmann 2019b; Insight Crime 2021a; Retberg 2021).

[33] Organizations can pursue activities related to narco-trafficking without necessarily engaging in vertical or horizontal integration.

groups, especially in production and transit countries.[34] In the online Appendix, we provide a stylized description of the business structure of transnational DTOs, which significantly shapes the drugs industry. We explain the differences between the monopolistic and oligopolistic business structures characteristic of larger DTOs (described in the online Appendix) and those observed in our cases, where local criminal syndicates operate with significant constraints given their weakness vis-à-vis the more powerful transnational DTOs.

The configuration of narco-trafficking activities in more peripheral markets for production and consumption tends to differ from those observed in counties where dominant DTOs operate. Different activities in the narco-trafficking chain function with greater degrees of autonomy. In a nutshell, macro-trafficking in and out of a country might be dominated by some organizations (e.g., international DTOs) whereas, micro-trafficking might be structured around distributor and retailer chains that operate with relative independence and across different locations. This system can lead, for instance, to territorial disputes among familial clans and gangs engaging in micro-trafficking at the local level. However, these squabbles tend not to escalate to higher levels in the narco-trafficking chain (Bagley and Rosen 2017).

Although contextual conditions influence all countries, domestic considerations drive them apart. We identify three main factors that push Latin American countries to bifurcate in terms of the influence DTOs exercise over criminal politics: (i) a country's competitive advantages with respect to narco-trafficking activities; (ii) the nature of the existing local criminal underworld; and (iii) backward and forward linkages to existing licit industries.

With regard to drug trafficking, countries differ in terms of their competitive advantages (i.e., location, market size, climate). These conditions determine their place in the narcotics industry. Some countries specialize in production, while others serve as transshipment hubs and export to neighboring countries or prime European, Asian, and North American markets. The size of each local market and the geographical location are also pivotal factors. Large countries with a sizable domestic economy that share borders with important consumer markets have competitive advantages. Such conditions have often paved the way for powerful DTOs to emerge – as in Mexico, for example (Osorno 2009). Conversely, countries with smaller domestic markets and located on the periphery of main trafficking routes predictably play a secondary role and, consequently, are less likely to produce powerful DTOs (Inkster and Comolli 2012). Colombia is an outlier, for it has a small domestic market and enjoys overt geographical competitive advantages, at least in proximity to large markets.

---

[34] Interviews by the authors with prosecutors in Asunción, Lima, Montevideo, and Santiago.

Its relative disadvantages, however, are mitigated by a climate conducive to crops such as coca and marijuana and access to the Pacific and Atlantic oceans (Camacho 2006; Llorente and McDermott 2014).

Countries' specific endowments for narco-trafficking activities are not necessarily fixed, however. In recent years, the expansion of synthetic drugs, which can be produced anywhere, has significantly altered regional production locations (United Nations Office on Drugs and Crime 2021). At the same time, the emergence of cocaine base paste (*pasta base*) consumption in urban areas in the Southern Cone during the early 2000s also reshaped internal consumption markets in the region's urban areas (Bergman 2018a). The availability of cocaine base paste increased, and its production became decentralized due to disruptions in the cocaine productive chain after criminal actors transitioned from operating large clandestine laboratories in producing countries to smaller, makeshift urban labs that were much harder for law enforcement to detect. The disruption opened the door for the massification of this highly addictive drug in underserved communities and its use as a currency to pay those employed by the trafficking organizations (Transnational Institute 2006). This trend created a new development: the proliferation of smaller micro-trafficking organizations in these marginal areas took advantage of cheaper entry costs into the business to profit from an expanding market. The eventual consolidation of these new markets also triggered increasing gang violence at the neighborhood level (Juetersonke, Muggah, and Rogers 2009), as well as a diversification of criminal enterprises into violent robbery, extortion, and gambling.[35]

Productive endowments and geographical location must be considered along with preexisting criminal contexts at the local level. In settings characterized by robust, centralized criminal organizations with deep societal roots that have permeated state and political structures, drug trafficking has often been a powerful booster of organized crime. Several authors point out that preexisting organizations structured around illegal activities can quickly adapt to new market dynamics (Moncada 2016). We have already alluded to the evolution of Mexico's drug industry in the face of changes, where relatively unsophisticated but pervasive criminal organizations with deep societal roots and widespread links to state and political structures (i.e., the protection racket) became formidable players with a transnational reach, coming to dominate the business and directly challenging the Mexican state (Knight 2012). Colombia is another interesting case in which the cocaine industry flourished due to the restructuring of criminal activities (the so-called *marimberos*) after the marijuana industry on the Caribbean coast collapsed in the late 1970s (Britto 2020). A bold generation

---

[35] Interview with high-ranking Mexican official, Mexico City, September 2013.

of drug traffickers, particularly the Medellín Cartel (Pablo Escobar, Gonzalo Rodríguez Gacha), who began as smugglers and marijuana traffickers, revolutionized the business (Gootenberg 2007; Duncan 2015b).

Contexts of internal conflict or insurgency may create ideal conditions for the emergence and/or strengthening of DTOs. The breakdown of order that characterizes these contexts offers ideal conditions for the business to flourish and provides these actors with unparalleled access to weapons and violence specialists (Keen 1996; Kaldor 2001; Cruz 2011). Colombia is one of the most emblematic examples of this: paramilitary and guerrilla groups took advantage of contextual conditions created by the war and became deeply embroiled in the narcotics business (Duncan 2006). In Brazil, the incarceration of local gang leaders along with leftist union leaders during Brazil's military dictatorship sparked the emergence of the CV, which combines an organized crime ethos with an insurgent discourse (Huguet and Szabó de Carvalho 2008; Penglase 2008; Insight Crime 2022). In settings with fragmented, relatively weak criminal structures lacking solid roots in society and influence over state and political institutions, the irruption of the drug trade has not turned local criminal organizations into powerful syndicates. In such settings, relatively small, unsophisticated criminal groups, mostly family clans, concentrate on trafficking, rarely venturing into sophisticated distribution networks along the narcotrafficking chain.[36]

Narco-trafficking also produces essential backward and forward linkages (Hirschman 1958) to legal enterprises, whose presence is also contingent on countries' specific productive endowments and competitive advantages. In terms of backward linkages, for instance, synthetic drug production requires chemicals used in specific legal industries (pharmaceutical, agribusiness, mining, etc.) which are usually subject to strict regulatory oversight. In the early 2000s, Argentina's weak enforcement of regulations on chemicals entering the country was pivotal in nurturing methamphetamine production in Mexico. Chemicals such as ephedrine, nominally produced for local pharmaceutical industries, ended up being shipped to Mexico from Argentina (and China.) Drug-trafficking organizations such as the Knights Templar and, more recently, the Cartel Jalisco Nueva Generación (CJNG) have engaged in this activity using chemical products that are legal to produce illegal substances (Ford 2022a). The commodity boom of the early 2000s (2005–15), which contributed to

---

[36] As indicated, in Argentina police organizations are deeply embedded in organized crime (Auyero 2007). This coordination imposes conditions on political and judicial actors alike; when in *equilibrium*, corruption helps to reduce violence as authorities profit from a wide range of illegal enterprises (Saín 2002; Dewey, Miguez, and Saín 2017).

neoextractivism in agriculture and mining and led to greater availability of chemicals throughout South America, reinforced this trend (Svampa 2019; Ford 2022a).

With regard to forward linkages, advanced logistics infrastructures linked with export industries (mining, agribusiness, fishing, timber) can act as springboards for international drug shipments to African, European, North American, and Asian economies. Food products are especially useful, as they typically go through expedited customs screenings due to their short shelf life. In addition to sea exports, increasing tourism yields a greater availability of flights for exporting drugs and importing the cash received from macro-shipments. Similarly, agricultural investments and the rising value of land create opportunities for money laundering through investment in rural real estate. Moreover, increasing prosperity has led to the development of dense internal markets for drug consumption, which can be vertically integrated into international networks (e.g., Brazil) or function autonomously (e.g., Argentina). It has also fostered new construction and further investments in urban real estate. Lima and the Peruvian coastline, for instance, saw a massive increase in the construction of apartment complexes and condominiums in the early 2000s. Real-estate projects financed with drug money also mushroomed in Argentina and Uruguay, especially in Punta del Este. The latter became a preferred location for money laundering and a residential hotspot for international traffickers. Besides luxury and tranquility, Punta del Este offered the chance to operate under Uruguay's (until recently) very permissive rules for offshore financial investments.[37]

Technological disruptions in legal markets also reshape narco-trafficking activities. For instance, in recent years, the expansion of social networks and food delivery applications created new tools for the micro-trafficking industry, especially for transactions targeted at wealthy urban consumers. According to our fieldwork in Chile, take-out restaurants, liquor stores, and informal (yet not illegal) gambling machines in neighborhood stores became focal points for money-laundering activities by local gangs. Tokens like Bitcoin, as well as the expansion of the evangelical church (especially neo-Pentecostalism) in a growing number of Latin American countries (see Smith and Boas 2020) also provide new avenues for money laundering. In the latter case, tithes (*diezmo*) are virtually impossible to regulate and oversee and have become a significant method of financing political careers, especially at the local level,

---

[37] Those features explain why, along with explicit legal omissions related to the import and export of metals, a country with no mineral wealth and no significant active exploitation eventually became a prominent importer of silver and a leading exporter of gold (Leiva 2008). Uruguay has also provided a springboard for money laundering through its well-developed (but highly suspicious) soccer player transaction market (Ladra 2014).

allowing narco-trafficking organizations and their associates to reshape local and (in some cases) congressional politics (Albert and Arellano 2018).

To buttress their business, DTOs often take advantage of existing criminal structures in places where they operate. Developments in the Bolivian highlands bordering Chile are a case in point. In recent years, high-end cars stolen in Chile were frequently exchanged for cocaine in Bolivia in what came to be known, in popular jargon, as the "autos X droga" business. Not every car smuggled into Bolivia is stolen in Chilean cities, however.[38] The Free-Trade Zone (ZOFRI) located in the Chilean seaport of Iquique, which receives used Japanese cars historically destined for Paraguay, also supplied (stolen) vehicles that were smuggled into Bolivia on a large scale in exchange for drugs. In Argentina, Uruguay, and Paraguay, meanwhile, traditional smuggling networks specializing in the production and distribution of counterfeit cigarettes and alcoholic beverages (produced in Paraguay) and counterfeit consumer goods (either imported from China or produced in illegal industrial hubs, such as La Salada in Argentina) have rapidly reconverted to new businesses such as drug smuggling.[39]

2.4.4 The Criminal Side: Incentives Guiding Organized Crime Actors' Interactions with Politicians and State Agents

In what follows, we briefly elaborate on the criminals' incentive structure, as it constitutes another relevant piece shaping our dependent variable. We assume that DTOs' primary motivation is profit and that conditions such as population density and state presence in an area are only second-order considerations. To minimize operational costs, DTOs have the following transitive preferences regarding their modi operandi. Whenever possible, they will seek to operate in places where the rents to be extracted are high and state reach is relatively weak or nonexistent. In such scenarios, criminals often benefit from politicians' choice to forbear. Nevertheless, standoff configurations are complex and costly, particularly in highly populated areas, due to the need to invest in public goods provision and/or a solid coercive apparatus to ensure the population's (and politicians') compliance with criminal governance. In addition, for certain organized crime activities such as drug distribution for local markets, rent extraction is directly proportional to population density (i.e.,

---

[38] The massive inflow of smuggled cars into Bolivia has been so significant that it created a political problem for the government of the Movimiento al Socialismo (MAS), which enacted several decrees (contested by the opposition and vested interests, such as formal companies invested in transportation) to legalize the so-called *autos chutos* (Anoticia 2 Bolivia 2021).

[39] The La Salada market is also frequently associated with human trafficking. (Dewey 2016).

the denser a locality, the more rent criminals can accrue).[40] Moreover, profit margins with international operations are also directly proportional to the challenges of moving products across borders. Such difficulties are usually related to the presence of patrolling or enforcement by state agents in border zones.

Therefore, when operating in densely populated and/or heavily patrolled functional arenas (e.g., ports, airports, major highways, and some border crossings), DTOs should prefer buying off and co-opting political and/or local and state authorities that threaten their activities (Durán-Martínez 2018). However, even if politicians and state agents seek to "crackdown" on criminality, this usually only increases incentives to bribe defectors (see Lessing 2017). Open violence, by contrast, is usually an off-equilibrium scenario and thus ends up being unstable and costly. Violence usually arises because of territorial disputes among criminal organizations, through turf and succession wars in which state agents and local politicians can and do often take sides, particularly in settings where law enforcement agencies and other security forces are fragmented (Durán-Martínez 2018; Trejo and Ley 2020).[41] Under certain conditions (especially in places where criminal organizations enjoy a dominant position), DTOs can benefit politicians and law enforcement by providing order and reducing the centrality and visibility of open violence. Conversely, in the context of turf disputes, conflict among rival gangs can have significant political costs for incumbents (Friman 2009; Magaloni et al. 2020).

Elective affinities exist among different types of locations and specific criminal activities that are either more or less predominant in each country.[42] For instance, if a country specializes in drug production in the countryside or has extensive micro-trafficking markets in its urban slums, the need for further

---

[40] For an excellent analysis of the logic of extortion, see Moncada (2022).

[41] The incentive structures of criminal organizations are thus different from those of classical insurgent and secessionist groups. The latter seek to displace the state to exert control of as many localities as possible, engaging in open military confrontations to consolidate territorial control; profit-making is second order, and only instrumental in financing further military operations (Lessing 2015; Trejo and Ley 2020). Kalyvas (2015) argues that organized crime challengers differ from insurgent groups in two crucial respects. First, while insurgent groups typically start operating in distant, unpopulated, and rough-terrain localities, organized crime challengers operate wherever significant profit is to be made from illegal markets. Second, organized crime groups do not necessarily seek to claim territorial control. Organized crime might invest resources in peripheral areas (where it can easily outcompete a nonreaching state apparatus) to exert territorial control via establishing para-states (Duncan 2015b). However, pursuing clandestine operations in areas actively controlled by the state might perfectly fulfill the needs of organized crime challengers to the state. Furthermore, given the nature of their profit motivation, organized crime challengers might move rapidly, switching locations, business activities, and organizational schemes in response to new production and market conditions.

[42] We explore those elective affinities in the online Appendix.

territorial control by narco-trafficking organizations to pursue those activities is greater. Alternatively, less territorialized criminal politics predominate in a country where the main activities relate to money laundering and macro-trafficking (i.e., exporting drugs produced elsewhere to international markets). The latter type of activity is often less politically salient and only becomes visible to the public if scandals break out. The former type varies in terms of political salience. Visibility might remain restricted if activities occur in distant or peripheral areas. However, when territorial control schemes break up and violence escalates in a locality, they might also attract significant public attention, thus becoming more politically salient.

These incentives notwithstanding, it is vital to remain attentive to criminal groups' diverse natures, strengths, and organizational patterns, as it would be a mistake to assume that all DTOs operate in the same fashion (Von Lampe 2012).[43] This variation has significant implications on the ground. For instance, organizational differences are salient in our cases, where cartelization and complexity are still rare because criminal organizations remain relatively primitive. Also, DTOs change dynamically depending on their environment (e.g., market distortions, relevant shifts in policies toward organized crime, international influences, etc.) (Albanese 2011; Bright and Delaney 2013; Pansters 2018).

2.5 Analytical Framework

International dynamics and national-level configurations shape criminal politics. The politico-institutional side results from the interaction between the international prohibition regime, geopolitical factors (e.g., a country's relevance for the US "war on drugs"), and local political and state structures. The criminal side, in turn, results from the interaction between the transnational political economy of drug trafficking and three local factors: countries' competitive advantages for narco-trafficking and what activity within this industry predominates (e.g., production, trafficking, money laundering); backward and forward linkages of narco-trafficking activities to legal enterprises; and countries' pre-existing criminal landscapes. These interactions are subject to contextual variation across cases and across time.

These interactions yield distinct *criminal politics* configurations depending on: (i) which types of engagements dominate politicians' strategies toward organized crime actors across jurisdictions and relevant functional arenas (politicians alternatively contest, seek rents, or stand off across time and space);

---

[43] For a theoretical account of the behavior of armed parties, see Schlichte (2009) and Crenshaw (1988).

(ii) whether principal–agent dilemmas are significant in the interaction between state agents (agents) and politicians (principals); (iii) how politicians structure criminal politics interactions (i.e., are they unified or segmented across narco-trafficking activities and the *places* they respectively engage?).

Figure 4 sketches our proposed framework for describing criminal politics in a given country and its subsequent implications. It shows that criminal politics stems from a complex intermestic dynamic combining powerful transnational forces that shape the drug industry on the one hand, and, on the other, contextual, local conditions that include a country's preexisting, long-term development trajectory, encompassing both state capacity and the nature of the country's domestic political and business structure and institutions. Such conditions are eventually reconfigured through feedback loops across time, especially when the illegal/legal ratio increases, thus amplifying the role of criminal politics in reconfiguring political and state institutions. On that note, we assert that criminal politics has two relevant impacts, which we will call first- and second-order implications. Levels of violence and corruption observed in each case are first-order implications of criminal politics. Second-order implications concern drug trafficking's more structural (but usually analytically hidden) impacts on a country's politico-institutional configurations and overall political economy.[44]

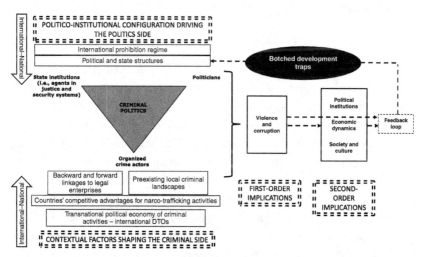

Figure 4 Explanatory framework for analyzing the causes and implications of criminal politics

Source: Authors' construction.

---

[44] We are mindful that first- and second-order implications are linked and characterized by a degree of endogeneity as both shape politicians and state agents' incentives.

Understanding the nature of criminal politics is important because, in the short run, it may negatively impact the violence and corruption observed in each setting. At the same time, in the medium to long run, it could reshape the nature of the state and political institutions observed. The economic spillovers and rents associated with criminal politics (e.g., via informal employment, economic growth, consumption, illegally generated social welfare, etc.) might also eventually impact other substantive outcomes such as socioeconomic development and political and institutional legitimacy. Analytically grasping the manifold implications of criminal politics is complex. In the context of this Element, we only begin to scratch the surface of those first-order (violence and corruption) and second-order (institutional quality and legitimacy spillovers) implications in Section 4.

3 Case Studies

Having discussed the nature and logic of criminal politics, in the remainder of this Element we describe criminal politics empirically by investigating our four cases: Chile, Paraguay, Peru, and Uruguay. We first discuss our case selection and empirical strategy. Subsequently, we explore the historical configuration of narco-trafficking activities in each case and describe its emergent characteristics. We close this section with a summary characterization of criminal politics in the four cases.

3.1 Methods: Case Selection

Due to the absence of salient and dominant large-scale DTOs in Chile, Paraguay, Peru, and Uruguay, our four cases might be thought of as "least likely cases" with respect to criminal politics (Levy 2008).[45] Our selection, therefore, illustrates both the pervasiveness and local variation observed in contemporary criminal politics. Our four cases also display different trajectories regarding the criminal and politico-institutional factors shaping criminal politics configurations. On the one hand, Chile and Uruguay have received scant attention given their relatively peripheral – but growing – role in the drug-trafficking industry. Paraguay and Peru, for their part, though much more important in terms of their role in drug production, have been overshadowed by cases displaying much greater visibility (Colombia, Mexico, Brazil).[46]

---

[45] An important consideration regarding the criminal side is that none of our four cases is heavily cartelized, as we show in the online Appendix.

[46] The online Appendix situates these cases in comparative perspective in terms of various available metrics, including corruption and violence, based on press reports for each case and the region.

However, each of our four cases presents different competitive advantages that make drug-trafficking activities more feasible and attractive. This variation is exceptionally important in shaping the criminal side of criminal politics and in determining the relative role of different narco-trafficking activities in each case (i.e., production, macro-trafficking, micro-trafficking, and money laundering). While every case has micro-trafficking, the size of each country's internal market and its relative incidence (more modest in Paraguay and Peru, more extensive in Chile and Uruguay) and interconnection with other drug-trafficking activities vary significantly. For instance, while Peru remains a key producer and exporter of cocaine, Paraguay is currently undergoing a transition from being a production site (especially of marijuana) to serving as a logistic hub, connecting smuggling routes from Bolivia to Brazil and the hydro-highway (which also incorporates Argentina and Uruguay as springboards for smuggling drugs via different transoceanic routes). Brazilian gangs are crucial players behind that transition. Meanwhile, Uruguay remains a prime financial plaza for large-scale money laundering but has also transitioned into a crucial logistical hub. Chile has also consolidated its role as a logistical hub while remaining an important market for micro-trafficking and consumption. In recent years, drug production (marijuana and synthetic drugs) has also increased in the country. Our historical narrative and contemporary assessment describe this variation and its implications for criminal politics.

Similarly, each case has specific politico-institutional structures, which configure the political side of criminal politics. Chile and Uruguay are conventionally thought of as having higher-quality, more stable democracies than Paraguay and Peru. Chile, however, is witnessing increasing levels of fragmentation in its political system and has become eerily reminiscent of the atomized Peruvian system. Such fragmentation manifests at the territorial level, creating significant challenges for aggregation and coordination across jurisdictions. Aggregate electoral volatility figures remain low in Chile, thus masking this fragmentation. Upon closer scrutiny, though, local politics is dominated by cults of personality, with leaders formally running under party labels but not engaging in party-wide "horizontal coordination" across districts (Luna et al. 2021). The cases of Paraguay and Uruguay show more significant levels of political aggregation at the national level. Although operating under different arrangements (more competitive and more programmatic in Uruguay; more hegemonic and more clientelistic in Paraguay), local politics is more aligned with national political structures in both countries.

State institutions in Chile and Uruguay are also usually described as having higher levels of infrastructural power, autonomy, bureaucratic capacity, and territorial reach compared to Paraguay and Peru (Altman and Luna 2012; Soifer 2013; Giraudy and Luna 2016). Nonetheless, our

Table 2 Political and state linkages' interface with the drug industry

State institutions	Political structure	
	Atomized, fragmented (local level does not necessarily reflect national level)	Nationally coordinated, less atomized
Homogeneous low quality	Peru	Paraguay
Heterogenous (greater quality in wealthier districts and salient functional arenas)	Chile	Uruguay

four countries also display critical (if different) weaknesses. Chile and Uruguay have significant internal variance at the territorial and functional levels. Wealthier districts and areas with greater importance in the eyes of states enjoy better-functioning institutions than poorer, less salient districts. In Paraguay and Peru, lower-quality state institutions are more pervasive.

We summarize this characterization in Table 2, comparing our four cases. We then speculate on how these political and state structures and each country's role in the drugs industry drive criminal politics in each case.

If we look at the two first-order implications of criminal politics (i.e., corruption and violence), outcomes also vary significantly across our cases. In terms of corruption, while Chile and Uruguay display the lowest levels of corruption victimization by police officers in the region, Paraguay and Peru are among the countries displaying the highest levels. These latter two countries also feature public sector corruption above the regional average.[47] With respect to violence, our four cases have been typically among the least violent in the region. However, Paraguay, Chile, and especially Uruguay, have witnessed an upward trend in observed homicide rates.

In sum, while they might be jointly considered least likely cases for observing criminal politics around narco-trafficking activities, our cases display a wide range of variance in terms of the criminal and politico-institutional configurations that should impact different criminal politics outcomes. The four cases also display substantial variance regarding the most direct implications of criminal politics: observed levels of violence and corruption. Finally, our four cases are ideal for testing our broader argument concerning the

---

[47] The comparative positioning of our four cases in the region is also consistent with annual estimations by Transparency International (2020).

detrimental impacts of criminal politics on development. On the one hand, Paraguay and Peru have been among the fastest-growing economies in Latin America during the last fifteen years. On the other hand, Chile and Uruguay are often perceived as positive exceptions in the region. In particular, the case of Chile has featured prominently as a model for promoting development in Latin America. However, we contend that these four cases each confront botched development traps due to the expansion of criminal politics. These botched development traps, while idiosyncratic in each case, are inextricably related to the recent evolution of criminal politics we describe in our case studies (Section 3.3).

3.2 Methods: Empirical Strategy

To substantiate our empirical narrative, we make use of primary research on all cases from 2013 to 2022. From 2013 to 2018, we conducted several rounds of interviews with state officials, politicians, and individuals involved in drug trafficking, as well as key informants in each of the four countries. During that time, and before the enactment of COVID-19 mobility restrictions, we also conducted interviews in specific localities across three of the four countries (Ciudad del Este in Paraguay; Casavalle and Maldonado in Uruguay; the southern area of Santiago and the Valparaíso region in Chile). We continued our fieldwork during 2020, 2021, and 2022 by tapping into secondary sources and investigative reporting about our four target cases and, where needed, other relevant cases in the region. Additional preparatory work was conducted in Mexico and Colombia in 2013 and 2014.

Our analysis proceeds in stages. We begin with a brief historical account, where we describe the evolution of the narcotics business in each country and underline how this history informs each country's position and comparative advantages in the industry. The account describes how the industry interacts with or shapes the nature of local criminal structures and develops backward and forward linkages to existing licit industries. Our description of criminal politics in each case concentrates on several dimensions. First, we analyze whether politicians engage in contestation, rent-seeking, and/or forbearance vis-à-vis criminal actors. Second, we investigate government officials' dealings with organized crime actors and ascertain principal–agent dynamics by asking whether state agents deviate from political mandates. Critically, the types of political engagement between politicians and narco-trafficking organizations described in Table 2, and the presence or absence of significant principal–agent problems shaping their implementation, vary significantly across and within countries.

Between- and within-country variation relates to the types of drug-trafficking activities that are more pervasive in each case, the types of functional and territorial arenas that those activities engage (relevant *places*), and the nature of political responses to such activities. Political responses are contingent on the political visibility (costs associated with corruption and violence) and rents (resources) that narco-trafficking creates for politicians. As such costs and benefits vary contingently, politicians often seek to implement a portfolio or "combo" of engagements with narco-trafficking organizations. In other words, they can sometimes seek to contest, seek rents, or forbear with regard to the same organization and place whenever the costs and/or benefits associated with narco-trafficking in that place changes.

More unified criminal politics might reduce the scope of possible within-case variance in a country. Therefore, we also need to distinguish cases where national dynamics are more prevalent from those displaying more atomized criminal politics configurations. In the latter case, variations across jurisdictions and functional arenas of the state are difficult to grasp through an overarching case narrative. Table 3 presents our proposal for describing criminal politics configurations across cases.

Table 3 Describing criminal politics: relevant features

Relevant features of criminal politics configurations	Research questions to be empirically assessed
Types of interaction between politicians and organized crime players (rent-seeking, contestation, standoff)	How is the combination of interactions distributed territorially and across organized crime activities?
Are there salient principal–agent dilemmas at play?	How and in relation to which criminal activities do state agents deviate from political mandates?
Are observed criminal politics configurations vertically and horizontally integrated	Are national authorities able to unify criminal politics across *places* and in relation to different narco-trafficking activities? Alternatively, do local political authorities deviate from national-level criminal politics dynamics and/or are sharp divergences observed across *places* where different phases of narco-trafficking occur?

3.3 Criminal Politics in Selected Cases: Historical Trajectories

To analyze our cases comparatively, and based on our theoretical discussion, in this section we succinctly describe the evolution of the narcotics industry in each country and underline how the country's unique features and comparative advantages inform the role of this industry. This historical account sets the stage for our analysis of variations in criminal politics and our four case studies. Based on our fieldwork and an extensive reevaluation of secondary sources, we trace how the interaction between each country's position and its competitive advantages – or disadvantages –related to the drugs industry influences the nature of criminal politics at the national level.[48]

3.3.1 The Evolution of Narco-trafficking

Paraguay

While illicit drugs have traditionally been important in Paraguay, the country has become a significant player in the narcotics business over the last twenty years. Today, it is the largest marijuana producer in South America and a strategic site for the transshipment of other more profitable drugs, including cocaine and synthetic drugs (ecstasy, methamphetamine, LSD, and 'tusi'). Paraguay enjoys a competitive advantages due to its favorable climatic and geographic conditions (Garat 2016; Insight Crime 2020).

Paraguay's narcotics industry goes back to the 1960s, when marijuana growers moved to the northeastern Chaco savannah region bordering Bolivia and Brazil. During this period, Paraguay also briefly played a role as a key transshipment hub for smuggling heroin into the United States. Following the shutdown of the heroin route due to pressure from Washington, Paraguay turned instead into a transshipment hub for cocaine coming from Peru and Bolivia destined for Argentina and Brazil (Simon 1992).

Paraguay's involvement in the drug industry is the result of several interwoven factors. The vast, unpopulated lowlands in the Chaco region, ideal for the cultivation of marijuana, turned Paraguay into the "cannabis breadbasket" of the Southern Cone (Moriconi and Peris 2022). Recent reports estimate the size of the marijuana crop at 5,000–8,000 hectares, primarily destined for the Brazilian market (Corda, Cortés, and Piñol 2019; Radwin 2020a). In addition to its temperate climate, Paraguay's strategic location has made it the main corridor for moving drugs west across South America. Producers in the Andean region, including Colombian DTOs and their Peruvian and Bolivian intermediaries, have

---

[48] We are keenly aware of how subnational conditions also play a role in the emergence of drug-trafficking activities. On the competitive advantages of this industry, see Thoumi (2003) and Shelley (2005).

for decades trafficked narcotics through Paraguay to the Atlantic coast, especially to the attractive Brazilian and Argentinean markets. For their part, Brazilian DTOs have gradually pushed into Paraguay in an effort to expand their operations into the Pacific Rim (Dudley and Taylor 2020).

Political conditions have also played a significant role in the evolution and development of the Paraguayan drugs industry. Paraguay first became an important country for the drugs industry during the long dictatorship of General Alfredo Strössner (1954–89) and his Colorado Party. Strössner structured a personality-based regime characterized by patrimonialism and widespread corruption and cronyism where the drugs industry and other illegal activities (smuggling and forgery) flourished (Simon 1992).[49] One of the most distinctive features of the Strössner regime was the creation of a sophisticated protection racket around the drugs industry and other clandestine activities (Garat 2016). This scheme, under which the Colorado Party and the military provided protection to drug traffickers in exchange for payments that financed many facets of the Party's operation and kickbacks to high-ranking army officers, exhibited a remarkable resemblance to the scheme developed by the Institutional Revolutionary Party (PRI) in Mexico (see Snyder and Durán-Martínez 2009). While the country's transition to democracy in the late 1980s formally ended the protection racket, narco-trafficking has continued unabated, adapting itself to the new democratic context in Paraguay. The role of the Colorado Party as the country's predominant political organization partially explains this continuity. As a result, a significant share of the country's GDP can still be traced to the underground, illicit economy (Moriconi and Peris 2019).

Paraguay's deep-rooted institutional corruption fostered the emergence of a singular criminal underworld. General Strössner's firm grip on power and, in particular, the involvement of the Paraguayan Security Forces – the Army – in the narcotics business inhibited the formation of major criminal entities with power and high levels of autonomy. Most criminal organizations grew under the tutelage of the state and were subservient to it. With the end of the dictatorship, sturdier and slightly more sophisticated criminal groups began to emerge, mostly related to micro-trafficking activities and located in strategic border regions. While new groups emerged, including the Fahd Jamil organization and Jorge Rafaat's notorious Rotela Clan – the most potent local group, created in 2007 – no local criminal organization has attained a hegemonic position. The most powerful nonstate armed group, the Ejército del Pueblo Paraguayo (EPP), a guerrilla group composed of perhaps 100–250 fighters which took up arms in

---

[49] Paraguay under Stroessner. best exemplifies the concept of a sultanistic regime (Chehabi and Linz 1998).

2008 but had older antecedents, only recently became embroiled in drug-trafficking activities (Saffón 2020).

Since the 1950s, Paraguayan drug traffickers have taken advantage of backward and forward linkages to legal enterprises to ship drugs within South America and Europe (Radwin 2020a). The transshipment of drugs benefited from extensive and well-developed commercial routes linked to the country's agribusiness industry (meat, soy, sugar cane). In this respect, narcotics-related activities were much helped when the country joined the Southern Common Market (Mercosur) – a free-trade zone that also included Argentina, Brazil, and Uruguay – in 1994. More vigorous commercial exchange among these neighbors also propelled the smuggling of illicit goods, including marijuana and counterfeit products (cigarettes, electronics, apparel).

Ciudad del Este, a bustling border town and free-trade zone in the so-called triple frontier linking Argentina, Brazil, and Paraguay, has been an important site for moving narcotics and laundering money. As this binding site attracted greater attention from law enforcement agencies – both local and foreign – following the discovery of radical Islamist cells linked to attacks against Jewish targets in Argentina in the early 1990s (Sverdlick 2005; BBC News Mundo 2018) drug traffickers moved north to Pedro Juan Caballero, the capital of the northern department of Amambay, in search of less conspicuous routes. This area has become critical for the drugs business linking northern Paraguay, Bolivia, and Brazil's Matto Grosso region (Moriconi and Peris 2019).

Transnational factors have played a significant role in the recent evolution of Paraguay's drugs industry. The rise of powerful Brazilian DTOs and their gradual expansion into Paraguay has wholly altered the country's criminal landscape. Until the early 2000s, most drug-trafficking activity in Paraguay was in the hands of local groups, many of which had links to Paraguayan security forces. The aggressive expansion of Brazilian groups like CV and PCC has shaken the local criminal underworld. Local DTOs have been hard-pressed to withstand the power of their foreign rivals. Reports indicate that the PCC's expansion into the Paraguayan department of Amambay dates to 2006, while CV infiltrated the region around 2013. Their presence has resulted in a more complex and volatile situation, with frequent clashes among diverse local and foreign DTOs competing for strategic routes and influence (Cerna and Peris 2018). While violence was initially limited to Amambay, it has spread to other departments including Canindeyú, Concepción, and Alto Paraná, where DTOs compete to control strategic transshipment corridors (Solis, Cerna, and Peris 2017). The country has seen changing patterns in the domestic consumption of drugs, which resemble those in neighboring countries such as Brazil and Argentina: drug consumption is diversifying beyond the use of marijuana and includes a higher incidence of cocaine and particularly synthetic drugs (tussi, ecstasy) (Shuldiner 2022).

Peru

Peru has played an important though often overlooked role in the evolution of the drugs business in Latin America, most prominently as the primary producer - alongside Bolivia, and more recently Ecuador and Colombia – of coca, the main ingredient in the production of cocaine (Grisaffi et al. 2021; Office of Drug Control Policy 2021). Coca cultivation doubled in Peru between 2014 and 2019 and grew by 11 percent between 2019 and 2020 (United Nations Office on Drugs and Crime 2021, booklet 4, 15).[50] As in the case of Paraguay, climate and location have contributed to the development of the local drugs industry. Coca constitutes an ancient crop commonly used by indigenous groups in the Andean highlands long before Spanish colonization in the early sixteenth century. Coca production and consumption are deeply ingrained among the peasant communities residing in the Andes Mountain chain, both as a means of economic sustenance and also as an endurance-enhancing substance used by peasants doing labor-intensive work in the Bolivian and Peruvian Altiplano (Cotler 1999, chapter 2).[51] The andean highland's unique soil conditions and humidity are ideal for the growth of coca bush, though the tropical Andean piedmont – *montañas* –in zones such as the Huallaga River and central Andean Huánuco is also favorable (Drummond 2008).

Unlike Paraguay, where the state took center stage and presided over the development of the drugs industry, the Peruvian state adopted an ambivalent stance, balancing its desire to avoid disrupting Indigenous traditions – potentially a contentious domestic issue – and growing US diplomatic pressure to join a crusade against cocaine. In his detailed study of the development of the cocaine industry in modern Peru, Gootenberg (2021) traces its beginning to the 1860s, when the substance was legal and widely used for medical purposes across the Western world, particularly in the United States and Germany.[52] Indeed, the bases of the contemporary hemispheric network for cocaine production, manufacturing, and distribution were built around the turn of the twentieth century, when coca and cocaine production boomed across Peru and

---

[50] The latest figures put Colombia at the top of the list of coca producers with 1,010 metric tons, followed by Peru with 810 tons and Bolivia with 312 tons (Office of Drug Control Policy 2021).

[51] On the evolution of the cocaine market in Peru, see Mortimer (2000) and, at the regional level, Gootenberg (2008, 245–90).

[52] The chemical process of transforming coca leaf into cocaine, crystallization, which transformed this product into a global commodity, was developed in 1860.

helped to expand agricultural frontiers in zones including Huánuco, La Libertad, Pozuzo (in the Amazon), southern Cuzco, and the Huallaga River.

The military regime of Manuel Odría, who briefly ruled the country between 1948–50, altered the previous laissez-faire position of the central state and joined the war on drugs, partly due to US pressure. The move meant changing its stance from tacitly promoting the industry as part of a veiled export-oriented development strategy, to active opposition through law enforcement. As part of its new policy, Peru introduced several punitive laws, embarked on coca leaf eradication programs, closed clandestine laboratories, and revoked licenses from cocaine laboratories. It also enlisted the military by creating a special anti-narcotics division within the armed forces (Gootenberg 2003). However, reflecting the government's recognition of coca's relevance and widespread use among rural populations, the Odría regime developed the National Coca Enterprise (Empresa Nacional de Coca S.A. ENACO). This state supervisory entity monopolized coca production and operated until its dissolution in 1999 (Glave and Rosemberg 2005).

During this mid-century period, more stringent controls on production and consumer markets pushed prices up, inadvertently helping to reinvigorate the sluggish cocaine industry. Unlike in the previous era when coca was licit and thus produced by legal laboratories, often under the supervision of licensed pharmacists and chemists, the drug business went underground. Clandestine, makeshift labs processing coca popped up deep in the jungle, especially around the Pucallpa region, whence crude cocaine was exported via Bolivia to destinations including Panama, Mexico, Ecuador, and particularly Cuba, which in the 1950s became the party capital of the Western Hemisphere and a magnet for drug consumption (Gootenberg 2008). This development continued unabated, prompting a mini-boom in coca and cocaine production, mainly around the town of Tingo María in the Huallaga Valley in northern Peru, which would become the epicenter of coca and cocaine production for many years (Gootenberg 2007).[53]

The drug industry's developments were inadvertently shaped by the failed centralization policy undertaken by Juan Velasco Alvarado's (1968–75) military regime, which was designed to enhance rural development. Seeking to incorporate vast zones of the country that lagged economically and had a thin state presence, Velasco Alvarado enacted a series of measures, including offering small land parcels to peasants, preferential loans, and subsidies for productive projects to people willing to move to unclaimed land in peripheral areas.

---

[53] Around this time, the Chapare region in Bolivia also became an important site for coca and cocaine production (Radwin 2020b).

When Velasco Alvarado's corporatist, state-led experiment collapsed – and with it, its lofty rural development strategy – thousands of people who had moved to these areas were left to fend for themselves. Lacking options, many joined the illicit drugs industry (Gootenberg 2008).

An especially intriguing aspect of the Peruvian case is that, despite the deep roots of coca/cocaine production in the country and its obvious comparative advantages in terms of climate and topography, no major criminal organization capable of dominating the business ever emerged. Gootenberg (2003) chronicles the existence of local clans, some linked to influential families in provincial Peru, that became involved in the business. However, once the industry entered a crisis in the 1930s and 1940s, these actors disappeared and were eventually replaced in the mid-1970s by a new generation of local traffickers – *narcos* – mainly in the Alto Huallaga region. At the same time, Colombian cartels seeking to harness the country's drug-producing potential moved into Peru and attained a dominant position, with local groups serving mainly as producers under their business model. In addition, in the context of the country's bloody civil war (1980–92), the Shining Path, a Maoist rebel group, entered the Alto Huallaga Valley in the early 1980s (McClintock 1988; Cotler 1999). Shining Path cadres gradually became enmeshed in the drugs business – despite the objections of the Central Command that, for ideological reasons, opposed this development –eventually becoming an essential player alongside local DTOs (McClintock 2005). The group imposed a revolutionary tax on coca paste sold by cocalero farmers and offered protection to drug barons (*traquetos*). Later, the Tupac Amaru Revolutionary Movement (Movimiento Revolucionario Tupac Amaru, MRTA), a smaller insurgent group, also entered the drugs trade. By the early 1990s, UN reports indicated that there were 61,000 hectares of coca crop in the region. Given the Peruvian highlands' proximity to southern Colombia, the Revolutionary Armed Forces of Colombia (FARC) and right-wing paramilitary groups followed Colombian DTOs in extending links to local producers in Peru, further raising the region's prominence (Felbab-Brown 2005; Carrere 2022).

The Alto Huallaga context changed significantly in the 2000s as the weakening of Peruvian guerrillas and the de-escalation of the Colombian conflict opened opportunities for local families or clans to reassert control over production and processing. Counter-narcotics operations also forced DTOs to look for alternatives (Obando 2006). Gradually, the epicenter of the cocaine business moved from the Huallaga region to the Valley of Three Rivers, Apurimac, Ene, and Matero (VRAEM) in south-central Peru, an isolated region with minimal state presence which is also ideal for growing coca bush. Although severely weakened, remnants of the Shining Path still operate the business alongside regional clans (Pacheco 2012).

Like other countries, Peru has seen a sharp rise in micro-trafficking and domestic consumption. An important share of this growth consists of synthetic drugs (Infobae 2022). However, Peru has not experienced a significant rise in deadly violence related to this business (Assman and Jones 2021).

Chile

Due to its geographical location and small domestic market, Chile has historically been a peripheral player in drug trafficking. However, its busy commercial activity, ports, and relatively developed chemical industry has given the country some advantages in production and transshipment. The Chilean state historically took a less tolerant stance toward drug-related activities, combating them head-on, which contributed to keeping the country a marginal player.

In one of the few existing historical accounts on the matter, Fernández Labbé (2009) traces drug trafficking in Chile to the 1920s (see also Salazar 2019). Much of the early drugs trade involved legal means: pharmacies and doctors prescribing drugs, particularly opiates, to affluent sectors. Other substances would enter the market later, including marijuana and cocaine. Accounts mention profuse drug consumption in urban populations enjoying a bohemian life in cabarets, brothels, and other nightlife sites. To the extent that its climate and topography are not particularly conducive to drug crops (poppy, coca), Chile emerged early on as a transit hub. The country boasted one of the region's busiest ports on the Pacific, Valparaiso, which was ideal for smuggling drugs into markets such as the United States and Cuba. The port of Iquique in northern Chile also served as a hub for drug exports, mostly opium smuggled from Bolivia. Another factor that made Chile an appealing drug-trafficking site was its robust chemical industry, whose resources were leveraged by international DTOs. As for the existing criminal landscape, Chile's drug business was typically run by individuals or small, independent operations with minimal logistical capacity, mainly acting as intermediaries (Fernández Labbé 2009). External linkages were thus critical, including with Peruvian DTOs smuggling cocaine and members of the Chinese mafia bringing in opium from Bolivia (Gootenberg 2008).

On the institutional front, the drugs industry produced corruption within police forces, which led authorities to task the military with certain law enforcement activities (Solar 2018). In the 1960s, drug-trafficking activity in Chile began to pick up markedly. While there is scant information available with which to quantify the growth of the industry, one indicator is that in 1964, during the administration of President Eduardo Frei Montalva (Christian Democrat, 1964–70), the Investigative Police (Policía de Investigaciones) created a special anti-narcotics division, the first of its kind in South America (Solar 2018, 54–55). Years later, the short-lived administration of Socialist Salvador Allende (1970–3) took a series of measures to curb drug trafficking, including more targeted law enforcement. On the international front, Chile signed the UN Single Convention on Narcotic Drugs (1972). While the Allende administration had tense relations with Washington due to ideological differences, its concern over drug-related activity led it to agree to allow a DEA field officer to operate within the country (Gootenberg 2008).

The military regime that toppled Allende in 1973 took immediate steps to tackle drug trafficking. In November 1973, only two months after mounting its successful coup d'état, the military junta presided over by General Pinochet created a special division – known as OS7 – within the police (*Carabineros*), which took over most narcotics-related operations from the Investigative Police. Determined to restrict and control social life to prevent potential challenges to its power, the highly repressive military regime effectively curbed drug trafficking (Policzer 2009). Severely curtailed in their capacity to operate, local criminal groups went underground, while international DTOs, including the rising Colombian DTOs, looked elsewhere to continue developing their operations. Toward the mid-1980s, after the most acute phase of repression receded, drug trafficking started to gradually pick up again, particularly in the northern part of the country (Solar 2018).

The end of the military regime and Chile's transition to democracy in 1990 inadvertently created more favorable conditions for the narcotics business. The newly elected center-left coalition (*Concertación*) was concerned to consolidate the new democratic order and prioritized reforming security forces to minimize potential backsliding. Solar (2018) argues that the new authorities spent most of their energy and political capital attempting to reform the armed forces and the police, including vetting officials involved in human rights abuses and buttressing civilian oversight mechanisms. These efforts, however, came at the expense of law enforcement activities, including narcotics, at a critical time when regional DTOs were gaining momentum (Solar 2018). Sensing a window of opportunity, transnational DTOs moved into Chile. Operatives of the Medellin cartel traveled to Chile in 1993 to organize operations and spent several months in the country without authorities noticing their presence (see Matus 1999). Three years later, Amado Carrillo, the leader of the Juárez cartel, spent several months in Chile and, posing as a Mexican entrepreneur, managed his multimillion-dollar business undisturbed from a posh neighborhood in Chile's capital (Televisión Nacional de Chile 2021). These infiltrations illustrate how the country was gradually being pulled into the business and how its law enforcement agencies were not prepared to confront this challenge.

Chile's growing attractiveness to international DTOs resulted from the country's economic success. Its steady economic growth and open export-oriented economy with a robust international reputation transformed it into an ideal transit hub for the drugs business(Dalby 2020; Sampó and Troncoso 2022). Rising standards of living, moreover, drove up narcotics consumption across all income sectors. According to the Inter-American Drug Abuse Control Commission of the Organization of American States, Chile had become the South American country with the highest incidence of marijuana use and ranked third in cocaine consumption by 2019 (Organization of American States 2020, 67–68, 141). Steep consumption of coca paste in low-income communities across the country has become pervasive, generating a host of negative externalities, including rising violence (Luneke 2021).

Uruguay

The Uruguayan drugs market can be traced back to the nineteenth century when an incipient consumption market associated primarily with bohemian circles emerged. Like Chile, Uruguay has historically been a relatively marginal drug market in terms of production and consumption, given its even smaller population and market size. To the extent that Uruguay became involved in this industry, it was primarily because of the influence of its neighboring countries. Brazil and (especially) Argentina. Uruguay's location as a buffer state between the two South American giants, combined with its long and strategic waterway, made it a suitable corridor for smuggling various goods, including drugs such as marijuana and cocaine, which made their way to the River Plate basin from Paraguay, Peru, and Bolivia (Tennenbaum 2018; Bogliaccini et al. 2021).

Uruguay's competitive advantage in this industry is related to the latest phase of the business: money laundering. In the early 1900s, Uruguay became an attractive financial and banking hub, especially for the Argentinean capital. Political stability, bank secrecy laws, and a comparatively straightforward and efficient system for obtaining fiscal residency in the country and establishing Limited Liability Companies (LLCs) have positioned Uruguay as a preferred banking and financial hub in the Southern Cone. This characteristic is critical as, from early on, criminal organizations linked to the drugs business identified Uruguay as an ideal location to launder their vast earnings. The booming tourism and real-estate industries, especially around Punta del Este, an internationally acclaimed and modern seaside resort, also contributed to Uruguay's appeal as a money-laundering destination. The Uruguayan state, like Chile, has combated drug-trafficking activities such as commercialization and transshipment but has been rather lax regarding money laundering, as it has sought to protect its valuable financial sector (Ladra 2014).

Uruguay became a preferential transit spot for macro-trafficking with its busy seaport, lightly controlled airport and airways, and permeable borders with Argentina and Brazil. In the 1980s and 1990s, especially, Uruguay became a significant departure location for drugs produced on the continent and exported via African and European routes. Like Chile, Uruguay's strategic position and reputation as a country with low levels of criminality and no connection to the drugs trade made it attractive for organizations seeking to export drugs to markets far afield, especially Europe. Uruguayan ports, particularly Montevideo, which in recent decades has been transformed into one of the most high-tech harbors in South America, has handled ever-growing volumes of freight, and this was seen as ideal for drug trafficking, attracting several powerful foreign DTOs.

While drug-trafficking activity blossomed during the mid-1970s, no important DTO emerged in the country, and organized crime was rare. The structure of Uruguayan micro-trafficking gangs is like that observed in Chile, where family clans dominate activities in their respective areas of influence (Leal 2021). Police reform, beginning in 2010, successfully curtailed police corruption and collusion with gangs, leading to greater and more effective enforcement but also territorial disputes among rival and aspiring new groups.

With regard to consumption, up until the late 1980s and early 1990s, micro-trafficking was scarce and highly concentrated in small social circles. During the summer, micro-trafficking intensified to supply the Punta del Este resort market. Gradually, however, internal consumption began to increase without attracting attention or creating visible negative externalities. In a pattern reminiscent of the dynamics in Argentina, this arrangement would be significantly altered due to the introduction of coca base (*pasta base*) in 2001–2 (Sampó and Troncoso 2022). The highly addictive substance brought in primarily via smuggling routes inundated the market, especially in low-income communities (*Cantegriles*) in and around Montevideo, prompting a significant health crisis. On the supply side, the emergence of this drug coincided with a steep economic crisis in 2001–2 generated by Argentina's economic collapse, which hugely impacted the highly dependent Uruguayan economy (Bogliaccini et al. 2021).

Rising unemployment, hunger, and desperation threw thousands of people into the drug market, thus contributing to the rapid rise of micro-trafficking in the urban peripheries of Montevideo and the interior. Violence linked with local competition by drug gangs ensued and has continued ever since: Uruguay has seen a steep increase in drug-related violence, which has contributed to a rise in the national homicide level (Ford 2022b).[54] Incarceration rates also increased steadily in the country, with Uruguay claiming the highest rate (408 per 100,000) in South America in 2022 (World Population Review 2023).

Toward the end of 2013, Uruguay became the first country in Latin America to fully legalize marijuana production and recreational consumption, with sales starting in July 2017. The liberalization of the marijuana market did not fundamentally alter the dynamics in the drug-trafficking underworld, as local gangs kept growing. In recent years, the drugs industry has continued its relentless expansion, partly because of the decision of powerful Brazilian DTOs to directly enter the country as part of their plan to expand their operations on the continent. This development has prompted a massive readjustment of the local criminal scene and, as in the case of Paraguay, spurred turf wars among competing Brazilian groups and between Brazilian and local DTOs. Security conditions have deteriorated, and law enforcement agencies have been targeted, including an unprecedented attack against the headquarters of the anti-drug trafficking unit (Dirección General de Represión al Tráfico Ilícito de Drogas, DGRT) (Assman 2020). Violence has been exceptionally high along the southeastern coastline linking Montevideo and Punta del Este, the most developed and economically prosperous area in the country and, as of late, in the sparsely populated northeastern areas bordering Brazil, where groups from neighboring Rio Grande do Sul (Os Tauras, Bala Na Cara, and OS Manos linked to the PCC) are disputing territory (Jones 2021).

As implied in this brief narrative describing the evolution and main contemporary characteristics of the drugs industry in each case, these four countries, notwithstanding common features, display some crucial differences in terms of the historical trajectory and current configuration of narco-trafficking. The online Appendix summarizes the main characteristics of narco-trafficking in each case and across different activities central to this market.

3.4 Prevalent Criminal Politics in Selected Cases

Based on the previous discussion and drawing on our fieldwork, this section examines current conditions in each country in terms of our dependent variable. Following our theoretical account, we present a stylized characterization of criminal politics in terms of politicians' interaction with criminals in different drug-trafficking activities, such as production, trafficking, and money laundering.

Paraguay represents an anomaly among the cases in our sample in that the configuration of criminal politics is remarkably uniform: a *protection racket*

---

[54] The homicide rate doubled from 6.07 per 100,000 in 2006 to 12.07 per 100,000 in 2018 before dropping to 8.5 per 100,000 in 2021 (Expansión 2020).

recurs across territorial and functional arenas. For this reason, we begin with some general considerations about this case, before presenting our comparative account.

As indicated, Paraguay's political system is characterized by the existence of a long-standing protection racket handled by competing factions within the ruling Colorado Party and dating back to the Strössner dictatorship. Paraguayan politicians' structure collusive and corrupt deals with organized crime players across the entire narco-trafficking business chain, from production to selling on the streets and money laundering. Those deals span various places and centrally involve Paraguay's traditional political parties, particularly the ruling Colorado Party, and reach top officeholders. Politicians have thus developed a complex and broad network regulating production and encompassing administrative order, particularly around strategic transshipment areas and smuggling networks (with Argentina, Brazil, and Bolivia).[55] Paraguayan politicians also play an essential role in macro-trafficking, stemming from their historic participation in the development of the crucial east–west smuggling corridor and their covert support of land-grabbing activities (especially with Brazilian and *brasiguayo* landholders) to launder vast sums of money from narco-trafficking (Garat 2016).[56]

This configuration is consistent with the country's high incidence of corruption and violence (low at the national level and concentrated in certain hotspots). Politicians and state agents are consistently bribed, often under a hierarchical scheme (from high-level politicians to state agents, although low-level corruption of state officials is also often observed). Such homogeneity, however, has recently been disrupted by the emergence and growing influence of the powerful Brazilian DTOs, which partly explains some early signs of *iron fist* policies, at least in some areas (Dudley and Taylor 2020).

The incursion of Brazilian gangs has fueled factional fights within Paraguay's traditional political elite. In addition, our Paraguayan interviewees consistently cited growing transnational dynamics, such as the DEA exerting diplomatic pressure and offering critically needed resources and expertise to Paraguayan law enforcement agents in exchange for their commitment to contesting DTOs.[57] The growing influence of Brazilian DTOs seems to have upended the long-standing protection racket that has bestowed relative stability to the country for decades.[58] Brazilian criminal syndicates are also altering

---

[55] Interview with Asunción del Paraguay, July 2019.
[56] Three Paraguayan prosecutors underscored this matter. Interview with Asunción del Paraguay, July 2019.
[57] Paraguayan Special Antidrug Prosecutors. Interviews in Asunción del Paraguay, July 2019.
[58] Interview with Paraguayan Prosecutors, Asunción, July 2019.

long-established macro-trafficking routes connecting the country with foreign markets (especially via the Brazilian border province of Matto Grosso). Brazilian DTOs have also infiltrated the country's prison system and attained partial control over some facilities (ABC Color 2022).

Having examined the Paraguayan case, we now present an analysis of variations in criminal politics in distinct phases of the narco-trafficking business for Chile, Uruguay, and Peru.

3.4.1 Production and Manufacturing

In Chile and Uruguay, marijuana cultivation has intensified in recent times (Lissardy 2019; EMOL 2021). In Uruguay, massive illegal plantations have not been a major factor since Uruguay legalized and began regulating marijuana production. According to our sources, legal planters practice specific irregularities (e.g., cultivating more plants than allotted per farm, cultivating some varieties with a higher Tetrahidrocannabinol (THC) percentage than the maximum allowed by the government, etc.). However, the magnitude of illegal production activities in Uruguay has significantly reduced, and prosecution by state agents has also declined.[59]

In the Chilean case, marijuana is produced locally in specific areas and communities. Authorities have responded in inconsistent ways to the activity: in accordance with a contestation logic, crackdowns against marijuana plantations are frequently touted in the press, including the use of drone-based technology to detect illegal crops. However, our sources emphasized that state agents are often bought by producers in what amounts to a *Janus-faced corruption* scheme.[60] On the other hand, in the Araucanía Region (and, more precisely, in the locality of Tirúa), media sources have reported how Mapuche Indigenous communities fighting for self-determination have engaged in intensive marijuana production.[61] The region has also seen the arrival of opportunistic organized crime actors, which has precipitated an acute deterioration of security conditions marked by violent clashes. Authorities have decided to withdraw law enforcement agencies from many areas in this region, indicating they have opted for a *standoff approach* (Instituto Nacional de Derechos Humanos 2021; Newman 2021).

In Peru, as Durand (2007) observes, the formal, informal, and criminal economies seem inextricably intertwined. Here, we predominantly observe a political discourse centered on contestation regarding production activities

---

[59] Interviews with two legal marijuana producers in Montevideo and Canelones.
[60] Interviews with two local notables in Chile's V and VII Regions.
[61] Several interviewees, however, claimed that this only applies to a handful of cases (communities) and is not widespread. Personal conversation with two leaders of the Mapuche movement.

revolving around coca. State action, however, is characterized by a rent-seeking logic whereby local state agents in charge of disrupting illicit operations accrue money through bribes, constituting *Janus-faced corruption.*[62] The difficult-to-access rural periphery where production takes place – along with the weakness, fragmentation, and volatility of the Peruvian party system – create significant principal–agent dilemmas for politicians seeking to enforce antidrug policies. At the local level, bribes also benefit regional-level politicians who collude with organized crime in a highly fragmented (individual) pattern (consistent with rent-seeking by individual politicians or local-scale political machines).[63] In producing areas, organized crime players buy the acquiescence and eventual cooperation (e.g., for the operation of airplane runways) of local military and police officers and, very often, local politicians.[64]

However, according to our sources, some significant differences exist between Peru's two producing regions: the VRAEM in the south and the Alto Huallaga in the north. In the Alto Huallaga, production patterns are often altered by more significant enforcement efforts, as the DEA has focused on this region to combat the activities of Mexican drug cartels, which began to rely on northern Peru as a production and shipment hot spot to the United States after enforcement efforts in Colombia displaced their activities to the south. The VRAEM, conversely, has less salience for national authorities, given its specialization in production and smuggling to southern routes (serving Brazil, Argentina, Chile, Uruguay, and eventually African and European destinations) (see Paredes and Manrique 2021).

3.4.2 Micro-Trafficking

Micro-trafficking dynamics, shaped by internal consumption markets and the type of DTO international linkages, vary in our sample regarding their stability, extension, and externalities (e.g., violence). These dynamics thus configure different types of criminal politics. Except for specific territorial hot spots (e.g., international routes through which personnel are compensated in kind, receiving the product, usually crack, to sell locally), micro-trafficking activities in Peru and Paraguay are widespread and display contrasting levels of violence.[65] Their internal markets for consumption are less sizable, more

---

[62] Gustavo Gorriti, interviewed in Santiago de Chile, November 2013.

[63] Former high-ranking official, Peruvian Interior Ministry. Interview, Lima, April 2014.

[64] Security forces control a significant share of the clandestine runways. Carlos Basombrío, former Minister of the Interior (Peru), interview, Lima, April 2013.

[65] In both cases, the national homicide rate is below the regional average. However, some areas display significantly higher levels of violence than the relatively low national average. In Paraguay, some locations have among the highest incidences of violence in South America. With 69 homicides per 100,000 people, the Department of Amambay bordering Brazil has

subdued, and governed by a rent-seeking logic (more hierarchically structured by political machines in Paraguay; more fragmented and atomized in Peru). While in Paraguay this entails a *protection racket* configuration, in Peru, it is closer to *Janus-faced corruption*, although a *standoff approach* is also present.

With respect to micro-trafficking in the context of urban poverty and marginality, Chile and Uruguay also differ significantly. Whereas in Chile, the situation amounts to a mix of *lip service* and *Janus-faced corruption* (by state officials and some local politicians), in Uruguay, *iron fist policies* were much more prevalent, particularly between 2005 and 2020 (Ladra 2014). In Chile, bribes cover entire police units (tactical brigades) and, in some cases, extend into local politics (mayors, municipal council members, etc.) (Luneke 2021). In this context, rent-seeking by state officials is shifting toward incorporating local politicians in rent-seeking arrangements, giving way to *Janus-faced corruption*. In both cases, the differences we observe in micro-trafficking structure in urban peripheries are consistent with established findings in the literature on criminal governance (Arias 2017). Contestation prompts an escalation of violence, an outcome we also observe in Uruguay.

In Chile, the combination of contestation and rent-seeking practices by state agents and some local politicians is consistent with more localized and episodic violent events, especially when territorial disputes ensue or state agents break previously established rent-seeking arrangements. The latter has resulted in a significant growth in corruption among police forces and politicians, especially at the local level. Chile, however, has recently witnessed a transition in drug-dealing structures at the neighborhood level, as a highly decentralized network of small vendors (who lack stable relations with macro-trafficking networks) has begun to concentrate in more hierarchical organizations.[66] These more structured organizations still operate at the neighborhood level but have drawn on strengthening family clans to extend their territorial reach by integrating or displacing previous – and more independent – vendors (Informe Especial 2019; Guzmán 2020).

Interagency competition among Chilean police forces and collusion between police officers from Carabineros and the Investigative Police and specific narco-trafficking organizations have consolidated a scenario of *Janus-faced*

---

almost ten times the national average. This violence is, to a significant degree, linked to micro-trafficking (Insight Crime 2021b). Similarly, in Peru, the department of Tumbes and Madre de Dios had an average of around 20 homicides per 100,000 people in 2017, almost 2.5 times the national average. Violence here is also linked mostly to drug-trafficking activities (Comité Estadístico Interinstitucional de la Criminalidad 2018).

[66] Interview corpus developed by researcher Pilar Larroulet during 2013. The corpus includes interviews with convicted micro-traffickers, both male and female.

corruption (Albert and Arellano 2020). Police corruption not only entails the creation of "liberated zones" for narco-trafficking, but also side businesses such as the sale and rental of firearms to micro-trafficking organizations. At the same time, narco-trafficking organizations have also infiltrated the social fabric at the local level, gaining influence and control of neighborhood associations, soccer clubs, etc.[67] This has created opportunities for collusion with local politicians and, in some cases, narco-trafficking agents have secured their election to municipal office. In some areas of the country, according to our sources, these drug-trafficking political networks have penetrated party organizations, with some national-level figures accused of having a "narco" political base (Albert and Arellano 2018).

In Uruguay – especially in poor urban peripheries – micro-trafficking has evolved similarly (i.e., gaining a hierarchical structure around family clans that exert a modicum of territorial control in different areas of the city.) However, since 2005, the government has enacted a police reform that has effectively reduced corruption and kickbacks, formerly prevalent at the local level, partly through dismantling compromised local police stations (Ladra 2014).[68] Centralized control, as well as improved recruitment, training, salaries, technological innovation, and strategic coordination, has led to a greater prevalence of an *iron fist* stance. With the increasing territorial scope and organization of micro-trafficking organizations, though, greater enforcement has contributed to increased violence concentrated in narco-trafficking hot spots (Queirolo et al. 2019). While several of the most influential criminal organizations have weakened due to targeted police operations, micro-trafficking continues to be prevalent among gangs that are less stable and less well-organized (Insight Crime 2018; Leal 2021). Overall, authorities react to micro-trafficking in underserved Uruguayan communities using a combination of *lip service* and *iron fist* measures.

In what constitutes a common pattern, authorities' stance toward micro-trafficking varies in accordance with income levels and shows significant inconsistencies (i.e., enforcement is lax in high-income neighborhoods). Authorities take a *standoff approach* as they are reticent to enforce the law against dealers with significant social capital, connections, and influence. Interviews with upper-class dealers in Chile underscore how class considerations make state agents look the other way and steer clear of seeking bribes.[69] One source, for instance,

---

[67] Prosecutor Antidrug Southern Zone, Santiago de Chile, interview via Zoom, June 2021, and personal interviews in Chile by authors (see also Informe Especial 2019).

[68] Tactical planning director of the Uruguayan national police force. Interview, Montevideo, July 2019.

[69] Dealer from a wealthy socioeconomic background. Interview by Renata Boado and Nicolás Unwin, Santiago de Chile, May 2021.

claimed that when he got caught with several grams of cocaine in his backpack, the police released him without pressing charges after his "blonde, good-looking mum" came to the station and pleaded for his release. However, upper-class dealers also admitted to bribing state officials who oversee parties and events where drug dealing occurs, which amounts to *opportunistic (administrative) corruption*. In the case of Uruguay, we observe a very similar pattern, and these entanglements might also include local politicians, whose campaigns are funded by people in business with dual interests in the legal and illegal economies.[70]

3.4.3 Macro-Trafficking

Of our four cases, Paraguay is the only one that plays a critical role in macro-trafficking, notwithstanding Peru's historical but often neglected participation in the development of the modern cocaine industry and the fact that macro-trafficking and smuggling have increased markedly in Chile and Uruguay. In Chile, smuggling networks utilized for macro-trafficking, especially cocaine, are active in the north around Arica, the border with Peru, and Altiplano (highland) areas bordering Bolivia. Busy seaports, including San Antonio and Valparaíso, have also been crucial macro-trafficking sites. In the last decade, Chile has also become an important route for exporting drugs from Latin America to Europe, Asia, and North America via the Pacific Ocean. These drug routes have extended traditional smuggling networks connecting the Chilean city of Iquique to Asunción (Paraguay) and Brazilian destinations via Ciudad del Este (Paraguay) (Pechinski 2021).[71] In Chile, we observe a mix of *iron fist* approaches, leading to frequent seizures and prosecution, and *Janus-faced corruption* by state agents. Custom agents and border police forces are frequently thought to partake in institutional bribes, which are usually paid at the local level (to specific agents and brigades who exploit principal–agent dilemmas).[72]

With regard to macro-trafficking, *Janus-faced corruption* by state agents is the predominant form in Peru and Uruguay. However, the nature of bribes and their implications for the political system vary. In Uruguay, where bribing politicians appears less prevalent than in the past, our sources indicate that state agents often engage in corrupt deals with smugglers. The country thus seems to have evolved from a more politically structured criminal politics to

---

[70] Chair and deputy director of state's anti-money-laundering agency. Interview, Montevideo, December 2018.

[71] Existing smuggling channels are allegedly used by Brazilian DTOs to smuggle firearms.

[72] Chilean Special Antidrug Prosecutor. Interview via Zoom, Santiago, June 2018.

a criminal politics configuration closer to *opportunistic (administrative) corruption*. With respect to customs activities, especially, agents told us that in the past bribes related to smuggling were more often "shared" with national-level political organizations.[73] Those resources could then be incorporated into politics via campaign financing, which continues to be laxly regulated in the country.[74]

In Peru, our sources indicate that organized crime narco-trafficking activities have sought to buy acquiescence and favorable regulation by bribing national, regional, and local politicians. This dynamic amounts to *Janus-faced corruption*. In this regard, our interviewees frequently mentioned the "narco-bancada" (a narco-related congressional cadre comprising representatives from different parties). Nevertheless, given the levels of volatility and the cult of personality in Peruvian politics, these kickbacks generally do not go to political organizations, but to individual incumbents and their local-level machines.[75] Even if administrative and political bribery are both common, they are less unified, thus remaining atomized and structured at the individual level.

3.4.4 Money Laundering

Every illegal activity entails the need to launder the profits. Local money laundering is thus pervasive and performed in most cases through local shops, real-estate transactions, and luxury consumer goods deals (e.g., cars).[76] In contrast to large-scale money laundering, small-scale laundering activities are usually carried out by neighborhood gangs and other local illegal actors and are challenging to detect in countries with widespread informal economies.

In our analysis, we thus focus on larger-scale money laundering, usually associated with more complex financial and business-architecture schemes. To the extent that large-scale money laundering is more sophisticated, carried out by highly specialized organizations, and targeted by enforcement at the national and international levels, it is not surprising to observe significant variation among our four cases.[77]

While money laundering is extensive in all four cases, particularly in the corrupt Paraguayan setting, Chile, and especially Uruguay, stand out. As a regional financial hub, Uruguay has become a vital money-laundering site. Here, money laundering is thus more politically salient than in the other three cases. Criminal organizations (and others) have taken advantage of the

---

[73] Customs agents. Interview, Montevideo, July 2018.

[74] On the characteristics of financing the political system, see Buquet and Piñeiro (2014).

[75] Special Antidrug Prosecutors. Interview, Lima, Peru, April 2014.

[76] For a good overview of this activity, see Ungar (2007).

[77] A somewhat dated account of this practice in the region can be found in Alba (2002)

country's lax financial system and stringent secrecy provisions to launder vast sums of money. The country's real-estate market, especially in Punta del Este, has also become very attractive to money launderers. At the same time, the agribusiness boom brought on by the commodity super-cycle has recently led criminals to launder their money in rural real-estate investments. Argentinean upper classes and business elites have long been drawn to the country for similar reasons, regularly investing their legally earned resources in the Uruguayan market. Moreover, lax regulations for Finance Investing Companies (Sociedad Anónima Financiera de Inversión, SAFIES) have created favorable conditions for money laundering, as DTOs can use private investment corporations and so-called fiscal paradises that are difficult to trace. Finally, soccer, specifically soccer transfer fees, have also been frequently identified as a prevalent money-laundering platform (Ladra 2014; Insight Crime 2018).

In recent years, Uruguayan politicians have acceded to international pressure to pass anti-money-laundering legislation and tighten enforcement.[78] However, our sources emphasize that there remains ample room for money launderers to operate in the Uruguayan market. These interviewees often tied money-laundering interests to the financing of political campaigns by Uruguayan political parties. Interviewees in charge of oversight agencies also frequently pointed to the fact that campaign finance regulations are weak and that money launderers operate jointly with legal enterprises. They also underscored that the available legal instruments for investigating money-laundering activities are, for the most part, limited.[79] Despite international and national lobbying to enhance transparency and oversight, advances in this regard have been meager and setbacks frequent. We thus characterize criminal politics concerning money laundering in Uruguay as a combination of *standoff* (with the rationale that money-laundering activities dynamize the Uruguayan economy and produce sizable and welcome welfare spillovers) and a *protection racket*. In the latter scenario, bribes flow from criminal organizations to politicians (often indirectly via campaign contributions made by legal enterprises and state agents).[80]

In Chile, we observe active *lip service* toward "simple" money-laundering activities (e.g., suspicious bank transactions and investments in luxury cars and real estate). In this case, however, class differences are evident and account for different enforcement patterns around money laundering. These efforts target

---

[78] However, the recently elected government led by the Blanco Party (Partido Nacional) enacted a law, *Ley de Urgente Consideración* (2020), that makes financial regulation and laundering oversight more flexible. It was issued by Uruguay's executive branch in March 2020.

[79] Interview with public officer in charge of transparency agency in Uruguay, August 2018.

[80] Interviews with two top public officers in charge of prosecuting money laundering and illegal political finance in Uruguay; interviews with an investigative journalist and a private lawyer with an extensive background in money laundering cases, August 2018.

small-to-medium-size micro-traffickers, who have only recently started to make their laundering schemes more sophisticated (e.g., through operating local shops, restaurants, and liquor stores). Our sources expressed a certain degree of frustration, as large money-laundering operations cannot always be detected due to the absence of legislation authorizing investigations into complex organized crime schemes, and because of biases in the reporting system – only a tiny fraction of the suspicious activity reports submitted to the Unidad de Análisis Financiero (UAF, Financial Analysis Unit), Chile's oversight agency for money laundering, target holders of "elite" and "preferential" bank accounts.[81] Chile's larger money-laundering schemes are thus consistent with *standoff* criminal politics.

In the Paraguayan case, our sources emphasized the existence of vast money-laundering operations related to the smuggling industry, real estate, and agro-business. As indicated, Ciudad del Este, a bustling border town and free-trade area, is a major money-laundering engine. The configuration of criminal politics in this area of the country clearly points to a *protection racket* scheme. In Peru, meanwhile, the atomization of illegal actors, the high informality of the economy, and the absence of large organizations have rendered money laundering very hard to detect. Our sources emphasized that *opportunistic (administrative) corruption* by state agents, especially in businesses related to construction and real estate in coastal areas, the country's most developed sector, is widespread and that eventual trickle-downs to atomized local political authorities are very common.

3.5 Stylized Comparison of Criminal Politics in Our Four Cases

Table 4 presents a stylized summary of our findings regarding the configuration of the drugs market and the characteristics of criminal politics in each case. A more detailed account is provided in the online Appendix. Our stylized summary is limited in that politicians often combine and switch among different strategies. However, the patterns captured in the table represent, to the best of our knowledge, the predominant configuration of criminal politics observed in each case at the present time.

While in some cases criminal politics displays a unified pattern across different narco-trafficking activities (Paraguay and to a lesser extent Peru), in others (Chile and Uruguay) we observe significant variation across activities. Those differences relate, in fundamental ways, to politico-institutional configurations observed in each case. Criminal politics around micro-trafficking and macro-trafficking might be operated by autonomous criminal organizations that engage

---

[81] Personal conversation with UAF agents, Santiago, 2020.

Table 4 Criminal politics configurations observed in our four cases across main narco-trafficking activities

	Production	Macro-Trafficking	Micro-Trafficking	Money Laundering
Chile	Janus-faced corruption (countryside, urban labs)	Lip service (northern border and coast) Opportunistic corruption (logistical chain)	Lip service (shantytowns) Standoff (wealthy sectors)	Standoff
Paraguay	Protection racket	Protection racket (evolving into mix of protection racket and iron fist?)	Protection racket	Protection racket
Peru	Janus-faced corruption	Janus-faced corruption Opportunistic corruption (logistical chain)	Janus-faced corruption Iron fist (shantytowns) Standoff (wealthy sectors)	Opportunistic corruption.
Uruguay	Standoff (but legal marijuana market)			Standoff

with politicians and state agents in different ways across locations. In more "unified" cases, politicians and state agents interact similarly with different criminal organizations. In Paraguay, national politicians can structure an encompassing approach that unifies criminal politics across activities and space: the protection racket. The latter is consistent with a nationally coordinated party system and weak state capacity. Politicians can subordinate a patrimonial state bureaucracy in this system across most functional and territorial arenas. In Peru, unification is by default. Since the political system is hugely atomized and state capacity very restricted, political–administrative corruption is homogeneously pervasive across localities, state functions, and with regard to different narco-trafficking activities. Low levels of state capacity in both cases also contribute to a standardization of limited intervention. As our findings reveal, a politically atomized party system cannot subordinate state agents, and thus rent-seeking and bribes are controlled by state agents. Eventually, local, and national politicians enter corrupt deals with organized crime players, but they do so individually, configuring an atomized political–administrative corruption across most relevant places.

In the cases of Chile and Uruguay, states with greater infrastructural capacity, politicians can selectively distribute state enforcement efforts across narco-trafficking activities, localities, and functional arenas. Most literature obfuscates this important distributive implication revealed by our case studies by focusing on one single dimension of the business (micro-trafficking) in distinct places (poor-income neighborhoods). For instance, in the cases of micro-trafficking in wealthy social groups and money laundering, Chilean and Uruguayan politicians decide (at least tacitly) to *stand off*. Macro-trafficking (across the northern border) and micro-trafficking in Chile are characterized by *lip service* criminal politics because state agents have enough leverage (due to political and institutional fragmentation) to exploit principal–agent dilemmas in their favor. In Uruguay, politicians' greater capacity to rein in law enforcement state bureaucracies has facilitated the enactment of *iron fist* antidrug policies in shantytowns. Macro-trafficking in seaports and the international logistic chain have remained less visible in both cases. They are thus more amenable to administrative rent-seeking by specialized state agents such as customs. With regard to production, which is more significant in Chile than in Uruguay, Chile's political and administrative fragmentation and the low visibility of production activities (they take place on rural sites or in clandestine urban facilities) have been conducive to the configuration of Janus-faced corruption.

In addition, in Uruguay and Chile greater state capacity in some jurisdictions creates more significant variance in local state capacity across places. Nevertheless, criminal politics in both cases is also driven by different political structures. For example, the countries display sharp differences in the micro-trafficking dynamics observed in wealthy areas (where *standoff* criminal politics is observed) compared with poor localities (where *lip service* criminal politics in Chile and *iron fist* criminal politics in Uruguay are observed). These differences reflect Chile's more significant political fragmentation at the territorial level. In Uruguay, *standoff* criminal politics with respect to production and money laundering, and administrative rent-seeking in regard to macro-trafficking, can be partially traced back to the pivotal role of rent-seeking by state agents with close links to political actors.

The empirical comparison of our four cases allows us to draw some conclusions. In cases in which DTOs are not cartelized (and thus lack a more vertically integrated business structure), at least, criminal politics configurations are critically dependent on politico-institutional configurations. The behavior of politicians and state agents with respect to the challenges posed by the expansion of narco-trafficking is thus pivotal in configuring currently observed criminal politics. In other words, state capacity varies across countries and within countries across functional arenas. It constitutes a critical variable informing the way politicians engage with criminal actors (either contesting or seeking rent via the credible threat of enforcement). Politicians governing less capable states may lack other resources and opt to forbear enforcement. Regardless of the political will to pursue law enforcement, however, weak states are limited in their ability to control significant territorial and functional arenas (Rotberg 2003, Herbst 2000). Weak states also confront the challenge of distributing scarce resources to cover an extensive territory and functional scope. The low quality of state bureaucracies is also pivotal in restricting (amplifying) the principal–agent dilemmas that lead to administrative corruption (by state agents defying political will) and patrimonialism (Mazzuca and Munck 2021).

The nature of party systems is also important. More centralized party systems with national reach offer national politicians much more leverage over local politicians. The opposite holds for highly decentralized and denationalized party structures, in which local politicians play a leading role in structuring criminal politics in the districts under their control. The nature of partisan organizations and finance is also essential. In general, party systems in the region have become less institutionalized, more fragmented, and more denationalized, even in cases with seemingly sturdier party systems such as Chile (Luna et al. 2021). Certainly, the nature of political competition in the system is also relevant. The contemporary crisis of party systems across Latin America has opened the way to outsiders, who might eventually challenge systemic players by leveraging discontent and political scandals (Mainwaring and Pérez-Liñán 2013). These representation crises shorten political players' horizons and often reduce cooperation among political contenders. These transformations promote political fragmentation, too, thus constraining the possibilities for unification by systemic political actors. Indeed, our opening vignette in Section 1 exemplifies this type of dynamic in the case of Paraguay. When factionalism began to grow within the Colorado Party, the shape of criminal politics in the country shifted (from systemic collusion with organized crime to a more fragmented configuration in which collusion and selective enforcement became predominant). When political fragmentation increases, the leverage state agents have to exploit principal–agent dilemmas also rises.

Table 5 (above) summarizes the configurations we observed across cases and shows their impact on criminal politics. When political cooperation is high in the party system, and politicians govern a relatively capable state, we observe that the supply side of criminal politics is driven by "systemic" politicians, who are relatively better able than their peers who govern less capable state structures to shape interactions with organized crime. This does not mean that political cooperation is essentially positive. Politicians can and often do cooperate in colluding with and benefiting from engagements with organized crime. When political cooperation at the systemic level was high, we also observed greater levels of unification on the political side of criminal politics, since systemic traits prevail. The opposite holds for scenarios in which political systems are in crisis. Here, reduced cooperation by systemic actors and challenges by outsiders constrain politicians' role in configuring more unified criminal politics engagements. Thus, the configurations we observed vary more contingently across places and functional arenas and do so under a more direct influence of state bureaucracies than in cases with more unified criminal politics engagements.

In sum, we began this Element by arguing that the expansion of narco-trafficking activities led to parallel (yet nationally distinct) challenges across Latin American societies. Those challenges relate primarily to the strengthening of criminal politics, even in "least likely cases" characterized by their relatively better politico-institutional endowments and by playing a more peripheral role in the global drugs trade. Party-system characteristics and state capacity, both slow-changing and path-dependent, seem to be critical in shaping the types of criminal politics observed in each case; however, criminal politics is pervasive across the board.

We have argued that botched development traps linked to the expansion of criminal politics can significantly reconfigure countries' (path-dependent) politico-institutional endowments in ways that constrain development prospects, even in countries that have so far displayed favorable trajectories. In other words, although the comparative statics we have described here point to significant variance across

Table 5 Politico-institutional factors driving the configuration of the political side of criminal politics

	State capacity	
Political institutions	**High**	**Low**
Systemic cooperation, legitimacy, nationalization	**Capable politico-institutional system (Uruguay)** Criminal politics is likely to be driven by politicians' decisions and can be unified. Principal–agent dilemmas are constrained.	**Political coordination of weak/patrimonial state (Paraguay)** Criminal politics is likely to be driven by politicians' decisions and is unified. However, principal–agent dilemmas are potentially massive and could eventually generate less homogeneity on the ground.
Fragmentation, conflict, denationalization	**Capable state lacking political coordination (Chile)** Criminal politics is likely driven by atomized/ fragmented interactions between politicians and criminals; unification is lower. Principal–agent dilemmas are massive, due to the presence of autonomous and capable state bureaucracies. Systemic corruption of state agencies is more likely.	**Weak and patrimonial state lacking political coordination (Peru)** Criminal politics is likely driven by atomized/ fragmented interactions between politicians and criminals; unification is "by default." Principal– agent dilemmas are massive, due to the presence of a weak and patrimonial state bureaucracy.

cases, the comparative dynamics we have observed across cases point to the consolidation of distinct (yet equifinal) botched development configurations. We elaborate on these findings and their broader implications in the final part of this Element.

4 Implications

Criminal politics linked to drug trafficking presents serious challenges for contemporary societies, some of which are more readily observable than others: measuring violence – counting bodies – is, after all, more straightforward than documenting corruption. As a result, available metrics too often inadvertently obscure significant constitutive elements of the drugs business because scholars focus on the industry's most dramatic and usually off-equilibrium manifestations.

We distinguish two broad series of implications that can be derived from criminal politics. On the one hand, there exist first-order implications related to the narcotics industry's impact on violence, corruption, and the rule of law. On the other hand, there are second-order implications regarding three broad areas: politics and institutions, the economy and overall development, and popular culture and societal value systems. Of course, to the extent that drug trafficking constitutes a transversal force touching so many contemporary sociopolitical, institutional, and cultural dimensions, these areas are inextricably linked and mutually influence one another.

Jointly considered, the first- and second-order implications of criminal politics, through different causal mechanisms, reshape countries' prospects for development and democracy. Although we do not explore specific mechanisms in detail here, we do hint at the distinct and multiple ways through which criminal politics relate to emerging developmental bottlenecks, which we have tentatively called *botched development traps*.

4.1 Violence and the Rule of Law

As we have emphasized, violence has become a distinctive feature of contemporary Latin American societies, and is deeply connected to the growing influence of the drugs industry (Bergman 2018a). Not only has violent crime associated with this activity (assassinations, disappearances, shoot-outs) increased, but DTOs have broadened their business portfolio and engaged in other activities (extortion, kidnapping, human trafficking) that also produce high levels of overt and structural violence (Vilalta 2020; Moncada 2022). Violence constitutes one of the pernicious externalities of the drugs industry, and has widespread, adverse social and human consequences, most of which fall disproportionally on disadvantaged communities. In one of the most influential treatments of this problem, Rotker (2002) notes how amid conditions of general impunity and ineffective state protection, citizens in low-income urban communities live in a constant state of fear. Time and again, the sources we spoke to during our extensive fieldwork corroborated how Latin Americans live in "the age of insecurity" (Davis 2006), deprived of their fundamental human rights and subjugated under sociopolitical orders dominated by violent, unaccountable actors linked to the drugs industry.

Another first-order implication of criminal politics in Latin America concerns corruption, the administration of justice, and the rule of law. While a deficient rule of law has been a historical problem in the region, often linked to past authoritarian regimes (Méndez, O'Donnell, and Pinheiro 1996; Brinks and Botero 2014), narco-trafficking has exacerbated the problem because existing, fragile institutions are simply no match for powerful DTOs and their massive corrupting influence. As the power and influence of the narcotics industry have risen, so has its capacity to compromise fundamental dimensions of justice, including policing (González 2017), the courts (Brinks, Levitsky, and Murillo 2019), and penitentiary systems (Roy and Valensia 2014; Willis 2015).

Relying on their massive wealth, DTOs have coopted state institutions to neutralize attempts on the part of law enforcement agents to disrupt their operations (Arias 2006; Koonings 2012; Duncan 2022). Following Pablo Escobar's famous dictum – "silver or lead" – drug traffickers utilize a mix of bribes and threats against public officials (police, judges, prosecutors) and others seen as a threat to their interests (journalists, community workers). Among state institutions, the impact is most vividly felt among law enforcement agencies within the criminal justice system that combat DTOs, such as the police, but also among prison authorities and even the armed forces when they are deployed in counter-narcotics operations (e.g., in Brazil, Colombia, Peru, Mexico, Venezuela) (Llorente and McDermott 2014; Lessing 2017). To the extent that drug trafficking has developed essential linkages with the licit economy – a process we have detailed extensively – it has also curbed state capacity to regulate many of its activities, as illustrated by extensive money-laundering schemes.

The erosion of the rule of law has impacted various countries characterized by different levels of development, wealth, and institutionalization (Giraudy and Luna 2016). Fragile states with limited institutional capacities have seen their sovereignty threatened by powerful DTOs (Hellman, Jones, and Kauffmann 2013; Feldmann 2019a). Honduras, where organized crime has infiltrated the highest echelons of power, even reaching former President Juan Orlando Hernández and his inner circle, is a poignant example of this phenomenon (Berg and Carranza 2018).[82] With respect to our cases, Peru has struggled to contain rising corruption, while Paraguay, a notoriously frail state, has been incapable of rooting out endemic criminality and has witnessed the creeping influence of Brazilian DTOs (Solis, Cerna, and Peris 2017).[83] But negative effects have also been felt by countries with relatively higher institutional capacities, at least at the regional level, such as Uruguay and Chile, both of which have faced growing challenges to security, the rule of law, and corruption (Solar 2018; Sampó and Troncoso 2022).

4.2 Political Institutions

Across the region, state bureaucracies and political systems are being fundamentally reshaped by externalities derived from the narcotics industry (Arias 2006; Albarracín 2018; Trejo and Ley 2020; Moncada 2022), impacting democracy and development prospects in several ways. These include political legitimacy and the nature of the political system, the evolution of institutional and state capacity, and the nature and dynamism of legal political economies. Criminal politics alters political institutions in different ways. On the one hand, in contexts where campaign finance regulations are lax or difficult to enforce, organized crime can gain substantial leverage by engaging in party politics and financing political careers. The cases exhibit important differences, for instance, in the jurisdictional levels at which this type of financing is more or less feasible. Those differences, in turn, generate selection biases regarding who decides to enter politics and who ends up being elected in different jurisdictions. On the other hand, in contexts where state-provided goods are scarce, criminal politics eventually engages in surrogate social assistance practices in exchange for local support (Arias 2006). In these cases, criminal politics help to undermine the credibility of politicians, political institutions, and state institutions. Eventually, implementing public policies and enforcing the rule of law becomes increasingly difficult for the state, thus leading to "liberated zones," where criminal politics might become entrenched.

Such dynamics are apparent in our four cases. In Peru, an atomized political and institutional system structures its relationship with criminal actors at a highly decentralized level. This creates a self-reinforcing equilibrium in which more centralized policies and institutional innovations cannot be implemented because they are stymied or altered locally. The country has ended up

---

[82] Hernández was recently arrested on drug charges and requested by the United States for extradition (BBC News 2022).

[83] In 2022, a multipronged operation jointly led by European, American, and Paraguayan authorities disrupted an enormous operation linked to Brazilian groups, seizing assets of over US $100 million (Rainsford and Saffón 2022).

trapped by its incapacity to aggregate beyond the local level, a feature also characteristic of its "nonparty" political system. This has led to an acute governability crisis whereby no leader or party can muster sufficient support for a stable government, a weakness compounded by endemic corruption at the highest levels and significant political polarization (Muñoz 2021).[84] In Paraguay, a political system once dominated by the country's traditional parties and their close links to the economic elite and criminal actors has been challenged by the arrival of Brazilian DTOs, whose encroachment has increased violence in strategic hot spots and in the prison system. In the context of a highly patrimonialist state, this disruption has increasingly rendered Paraguayan elites and state agents less able to keep the "system" under their control. The current situation in Paraguay resembles Mexico when its PRI-run "plaza system" began to crack, opening the way for rising violence, although with apparent differences regarding the magnitude and scope of violence and economic margins.

In Chile, one of the effects of the political and social crisis of 2019 has been to increase the politicization of social privilege, not only regarding socioeconomic status but also in terms of access to civil citizenship rights (i.e., fair treatment by police forces and the justice system). Against that backdrop, narratives that portray politicians, state agents, and social elites as corrupt perpetrators of abuse against low-income sectors have gained traction. These narratives serve to undermine political and institutional legitimacy to the point of rendering the state increasingly unable to efficiently regulate social interactions in a significant portion of its territory. This, in turn, has opened up opportunities for criminal enterprises to expand. An incremental process of institutional weakening linked to growing corruption – often at high levels – low morale, and dwindling resources against the backdrop of ever more powerful DTOs has weakened the capacity of the state to enforce the rule of law and has had a deep impact on security conditions in the country (Guzmán 2020). Such conditions were worsened by the devastating economic and social effects of the COVID-19 pandemic (Luna 2021).

In Uruguay, the 2005 election to power of a nontraditional party (the Frente Amplio) paved the way for police reform and the legalization of marijuana production and consumption. Police reform broke collusive local pacts between agents and criminals, helping to centralize and coordinate enforcement. Greater enforcement led to more significant fragmentation among neighborhood gangs and an upsurge in incarceration rates. However, as in Chile, enforcement is uneven, with authorities cracking down on poor areas while being lenient or

---

[84] For an analysis of this pattern at the regional level, see (Carothers and Feldmann 2021).

negligent in wealthy districts. Moreover, authorities have made advances in implementing measures to control financial activities that are pivotal for money laundering. However, the Uruguayan political system has been hesitant to regulate the influence of money in politics, and has one of the weakest campaign oversight systems in the region. The country has also held back on establishing a transparency office with the capacity to actively oversee and prosecute illegal enrichment by state agents and elected officials. This omission is particularly glaring at a time when Uruguay has become a privileged location for the transshipment of massive amounts of drugs to Europe as well as a hot spot for money laundering in the region. The 2022 political scandal emerging from the "Astesiano" and "narco-passport" cases has already implicated top police officials in the country while bringing to light extensive corruption networks linking illegal economy operators, legal businesses, state agents, and politically salient figures (La Diaria 2022).

4.3 The Economy

Another set of second-order implications concerns the drug industry's impact on the formal economy and overall development prospects. As our analysis has shown, drug trafficking has profound implications on how contemporary Latin American economies function, creating multiple forward and backward linkages to legal enterprises and economic processes. Like many other highly demanded commodities, illegal drugs create wealth and investment capital, promoting a range of economic spillovers (e.g., growth, jobs, consumption, trade). The economic impact of drug trafficking is relatively more significant than other activities, especially where alternative economic enterprises and labor opportunities for the vast majority of the population are scarce. In such a context, the informal sector and illegal enterprises emerge as one of the few available economic alternatives for people to prosper and pursue social mobility. As indicated, while we lack precise numbers, economists estimate that the drugs industry makes up a significant and growing share of the overall economy for most Latin American countries. More importantly for our argument, over time this illicit business develops significant linkages across a range of areas in the formal economy, feeding off them and/or propping them up. In other words, this industry's influence is much more comprehensive than has generally been thought, as drug-related wealth contributes to many economic activities. Indeed, for many Latin American states, the drugs industry constitutes an indirect but highly needed source of revenue and foreign currency, without which many disadvantaged communities probably could not survive economically in profoundly unequal societies.

4.4 Society and Culture

Drug trafficking is also having a host of sociocultural impacts. In contexts where states have failed to provide public goods (e.g., security, justice, infrastructure) and thus lost legitimacy vis-à-vis their multiple challengers, crime has emerged as a subaltern social mobility vehicle across the region (Feldmann and Luna 2022).[85] This pattern has been reinforced by a consumerist society wherein, confronted by persistent structural inequalities and restricted upward mobility, people see drug trafficking as one of the few options available to access highly desired and status-enhancing goods (United Nations Development Programme 2013). Narco-trafficking has also become ingrained in common expressions associated with popular-culture industries, such as entertainment and sports like soccer. Our sources in each country, as well as extensive investigative journalism, document such interactions, including neighborhood soccer fields becoming privileged sites for drug dealing, soccer-hooligan organizations engaging in drug distribution (often taking place during matches), and the use of soccer transfers for money-laundering purposes. In Chile, soccer gangs have also provided campaign assistance to political candidates while participating in social protests and riots (Guarello 2021).

The nature of this relationship between soccer, narco-trafficking actors, and politics varies across countries. Whereas in Paraguay it has a top-down structure (i.e., run by party leaders who control nationwide machines that reach the local level), in Peru the system is wholly atomized, with deals struck by local and regional authorities and local criminal structures. The situation in Chile approximates the Peruvian one in that it has begun to influence national party structures. In Uruguay, most deals are secretly realized through party financing by legal enterprises with obscure ties to criminal activities.

The entertainment industry has also consolidated strong linkages with drug trafficking, providing opportunities for trafficking and extensive money laundering. Moreover, narco-culture expressions have also begun influencing societal value systems and cultural orientations. Emerging urban artists in Chile

---

[85] A striking commonality found by the authors during fieldwork in diverse countries over the years is the total lack of trust disadvantaged communities have in the state. After years of abusive interactions with its representatives (the police, the justice system), citizens do not expect anything from the state and prefer to steer clear of it, even if this means being subjected to criminal-led orders.

have adapted reggaetón to local culture.[86] In Chile, the narco culture, which portrays extravagant lifestyles and idealizes consumerism, coupled with the normalization of sexism and violence, not only primes criminal activities as a legitimate, rapidly rewarding mechanism for upward social mobility, but also legitimates criminal activities as a defiant tactic against abusive social elites, their repressive forces (the police), and traditional politicians. The influence of this value system is readily apparent in surveys with citizens who dwell on the urban margins where alternative vehicles for social mobility have proven more efficient than traditional mechanisms, such as pursuing a formal education. This cultural shift has occurred in tandem with challenges (as in Chile) to traditional political systems, which mass protests and rioting have weakened.

4.5 Research Agenda

In recent years, the "scaling down" of the unit of analysis has arguably yielded great analytical benefits. In our field, it has greatly helped to enhance our understanding of the relationship between nonstate actors of a criminal nature and the state and the impact this relationship has on governance (Giraudy, Moncada, and Snyder 2019). By selecting local violent/corrupt hot spots, however, the criminal governance literature downplays the multilevel nature of organized crime, its configuration at the national level and, more broadly, its impact at the aggregate sociopolitical level. Precise causal inferences – based on painstaking fieldwork research at the local level, often across multi-country research designs – articulated by the criminal governance literature have, in our view, come at the expense of selection bias. For understandable reasons, the literature has traded methodological and empirical rigor for scope by circumscribing – at least by default – organized crime dynamics within exclusively local scenarios (see Feldmann and Luna 2022). This limited scope has also, by default, stigmatized poor and marginal localities as the sole loci of organized crime. Scaling down has also meant artificially separating legal and illegal realms in the study of contemporary societies. However, as Andreas (1998) argues, legal and illegal spheres in society are coconstituted and in constant flux.

Criminal politics directly impacts the legal political economy of development, shapes the nature of state institutions, and penetrates pivotal organizations at the national level such as political parties. In such a context, we argue that "scaling up" seems critical to advance future research. By proposing the concept of criminal politics and by engaging in a preliminary mapping of its central dynamics in four countries that have thus far been overlooked in the specialized

---

[86] See Chill E (2018); Ignacio (2018).

literature, we are contributing to a broader understanding of this phenomenon. Even if the negative externalities of the drugs industry (violence, corruption, state capture) are not readily observable and easy to measure, drug-related activities are homogeneously present (and sometimes dominant) in every society and across multiple social realms. Critically, criminality linked to this industry not only occurs in impoverished urban margins; its primary activities may take place elsewhere. Organized crime yields significantly higher profits in wealthier areas (both at home and abroad), border zones, and semi-urban and rural areas with high-profit productive activities (mining, agriculture) and resource exploitation (mining, timber) that criminal organizations often seek to penetrate and control (Idler 2019; Duncan 2022). Similarly, organized crime impacts the economies of marginal sectors and across-the-board economic activities, including real estate, industrial production, and the financial market (Thoumi 2003).

Because organized crime is so ubiquitous across local and national socioeconomic spheres, politics, and state institutions, we attempted to scale up to meso and macro levels to gain a more comprehensive view of the issue and its implications. Such an analytical move, we believe, can leverage essential lessons that can be drawn from the literature on criminal governance at the local level and thus help to bridge different levels of analysis (micro, meso, macro). This methodological move has successfully been attempted in the civil war literature (Balcells and Justino 2014). Scaling up is not straightforward, however. Researching opaque criminal politics will not necessarily produce definitive and well-crystallized descriptions and causal inferences. The local and frequently atomized nature of criminal politics configurations across places also renders generalizations tentative, at best.

This Element has shown some of the limitations of this approach in terms of the tentative nature of the findings and conclusions. However, we firmly believe that researching important social phenomena should take priority over pursuing methodological fads, hunting for causal inferences, or accessing readily available data. We thus hope the analytical framework and the preliminary evidence introduced in this Element will help scholars embrace the challenges and theoretical promise of researching criminal politics and its multiple implications for the politics of development.

References

ABC Color. 2022. "PCC tiene más de mil soldados en las cárceles de Paraguay," July 24. www.abc.com.py/policiales/2022/07/24/pcc-tiene-mas-de-1000-soldados-en-las-principales-carceles-de-paraguay/.

Acemoglu, Daron, and James A. Robinson. 2019. *The Narrow Corridor: States, Societies, and the Fate of Liberty*. New York: Penguin Publishers.

Acemoglu, Daron, Simon Johnson, and James A. Robinson. 2005. "Institutions as a Fundamental Cause of Long-Run Growth." In *Handbook of Economic Growth*, edited by Philippe Aghion and Steven N. Durlauf, 1385–1472. Amsterdam: Elsevier.

Alba, Ricardo M. 2002. "Evolution of Methods of Money Laundering in Latin America." *Journal of Financial Crime* 10 (2): 137–40.

Albanese, Jay. 2000. "The Causes of Organized Crime: Do Criminals Organize around Opportunities for Crime or Do Criminal Opportunities Create New Offenders?" *Journal of Contemporary Criminal Justice* 16 (4): 409–23.

2011. *Transnational Crime and the 21st Century: Criminal, Enterprise, Corruption and Opportunity*. Oxford: Oxford University Press.

Albarracín, Juan. 2018. "Criminalized Electoral Politics in Brazilian Urban Peripheries." *Crime, Law and Social Change* 69 (4): 553–75.

Albarracín, Juan, and Nicholas Barnes. 2020. "Criminal Violence in Latin America." *Latin American Research Review* 55 (2): 397–406.

Albert, Catalina, and Alberto Arellano. 2018. "Las estrategias que usan los narcos mayoristas para lavar dinero y corromper funcionarios." *CIPER Chile*, August 17. www.ciperchile.cl/2018/08/17/las-estrategias-que-usan-los-narco-mayoristas-para-lavar-dinero-y-corromper-funcionarios/.

2020. "La arremetida sin control del narcotráfico en Chile." *CIPER Chile*, August 16. www.ciperchile.cl/2018/08/16/la-arremetida-sin-control-del-narcotrafico-en-chile/.

Altman, David, and Juan Pablo Luna. 2012. "Introducción: El Estado latinoamericano en su laberinto." *Revista de Ciencia Política* 32 (3): 521–43.

Andreas, Peter. 1998. "Smuggling Wars: Law Enforcement and Law Evasion in a Changing World." *Transnational Organized Crime* 4 (2): 79–90.

2019. "Drugs and War: What Is the Relationship?" *Annual Review of Political Science* 22 (3): 1–23.

Andreas, Peter, and Ethan A. Nadelmann. 2008. *Policing the Globe: Criminalization and Crime Control in International Relations*. Oxford: Oxford University Press.

Anoticia 2 Bolivia. 2021. "El MAS alista ley para nacionalizar vehículos chutos, con cobros del 50%," July 8. www.anoticia2.com/2020/07/el-mas-alista-ley-para-nacionalizar.html.

Arias, Desmond. 2006. *Drugs and Democracy in Rio de Janeiro: Trafficking, Social Networks, and Public Security.* Chapel Hill: University of North Carolina Press.

2017. *Criminal Enterprises and Governance in Latin America and the Caribbean.* Cambridge: Cambridge University Press.

Arias, Desmond, and Daniel M. Goldstein (eds.). 2010. *Violent Democracies in Latin America.* Durham, NC: Duke University Press.

Arjona, Ana, Nelson Kasfir, and Zachariah Mampilly (eds.). 2015. *Rebel Governance in Civil War.* Cambridge: Cambridge University Press.

Assman, Parker. 2020. "Brazen Murder of Soldiers Latest Incident to Raise Alarm in Uruguay." *Insight Crime*, June 5. https://insightcrime.org/news/brief/brazen-murder-latest-alarm-uruguay/.

Assman, Parker, and Katie Jones. 2021. "InSight Crime's 2020 Homicide Round-Up." *Insight Crime*, February 1. https://insightcrime.org/news/insight-crimes-2021-homicide-round-up/.

Auyero, Javier. 2007. *Routine Politics and Violence in Argentina: The Grey Zone of State Power.* Cambridge: Cambridge University Press.

Auyero, Javier, and Katherine Sobering (eds.). 2019. *The Ambivalent State: Police–Criminal Collusion at the Urban Margins.* Oxford: Oxford University Press.

Bagley, Bruce, and Jonathan D. Rosen (eds.). 2017. *Drug Trafficking, Organized Crime, and Violence in the Americas Today.* Gainesville: University of Florida Press.

Balcells, Laia, and Patricia Justino. 2014. "Bridging Micro and Macro Approaches on Civil Wars and Political Violence: Issues, Challenges, and the Way Forward." *Journal of Conflict Resolution* 58 (8): 1343–59.

Barnes, Nicholas. 2017. "Criminal Politics: An Integrated Approach to the Study of Organized Crime, Politics, and Violence." *Perspectives on Politics* 15 (4): 967–87.

BBC News. 2022. "Juan Orlando Hernández: Police Arrest Honduran Ex-Leader on Drugs Charges," February 15. www.bbc.com/news/world-latin-america-60387156.

BBC News Mundo. 2018. "Brasil: arrestan en la triple frontera a Assad Ahmad Barakat, 'tesorero' del grupo radical Hezbolá y uno de los hombres más buscados por Estados Unidos," September 23. www.bbc.com/mundo/noticias-america-latina-45616776.

Benítez, Raúl. 2014. "Mexico–Colombia: U.S. Assistance and the Fight against Organized Crime." In *One Goal, Two Struggles: Confronting Crime and*

Violence in Colombia and Mexico, edited by Cynthia Arnson and Eric Olson, 47–70. Washington, DC: Wilson Center.

Berg, Louis Alexandre, and Marlon Carranza. 2018. "Organized Criminal Violence and Territorial Control: Evidence from Northern Honduras." *Journal of Peace Research* 55 (5): 566–81.

Bergman, Marcelo. 2018a. *More Money, More Crime: Prosperity and Rising Crime in Latin America*. Oxford: Oxford University Press.

2018b. *Illegal Drugs, Drug Trafficking and Violence in Latin America*. Cham: Springer.

Bewley-Taylor, David. 2012. *International Drug Control: Consensus Fractures*. Cambridge: Cambridge University Press.

Biondi, Karina. 2016. *Sharing This Walk: An Ethnography of Prison Life and the PCC in Brazil*. Chapel Hill: University of North Carolina Press.

Bogliaccini, Juan, Diego Pereira, Juan Ignacio Pereira, Cecilia Giambruno, and Ignacio Borba. 2021. "Tackling Drug-Lords in a Nascent Market: Raids and Drug Crime in Uruguay." *Criminal Justice Policy Review* 33 (4): 351–72.

Boone, Catherine. 2012. "Territorial Politics and the Reach of the State: Unevenness by Design." *Revista de Ciencia Política* 32 (3): 623–41.

Bright, David A., and Jordan J. Delaney. 2013. "Evolution of a Drug Trafficking Network: Mapping Changes in Network Structure and Function Across Time." *Global Crime* 14 (2–3): 238–60.

Brinks, Daniel, and Sandra Botero. 2014. "Inequality and the Rule of Law: Ineffective Rights in Latin American Democracies." In *Reflections on Uneven Democracies: The Legacy of Guillermo O'Donnell*, edited by Daniel Brinks, Marcelo Leiras, and Scott Mainwaring, 214–39. Baltimore, MD: Johns Hopkins University Press.

Brinks, Daniel, Steven Levitsky, and María Victoria Murillo. 2019. *Understanding Institutional Weakness*. Elements in Politics and Society in Latin America Series. New York: Cambridge University Press.

Britto, Lina. 2020. *Marihuana Boom: The Rise and Fall of Colombia's First Drug Paradise*. Berkeley: University of California Press.

Bruinsma, Gerben, and Wim Bernasco. 2004. "Criminal Groups and Transnational Illegal Markets." *Crime, Law and Social Change* 41 (1): 79–94.

Buquet, Daniel, and Rafael Piñeiro. 2014. "La consolidación de un nuevo sistema de partidos en Uruguay." *Debates* 8 (1): 127–48.

Calderoni, Francesco. 2012. "The Structure of Drug Trafficking Mafias: The 'Ndrangheta' and Cocaine." *Crime, Law and Social Change* 58 (3): 321–49.

Camacho, Álvaro. 2006. De narcos, paracracias y mafias. In *La encrucijada: Colombia en el siglo XXI*, edited by Francisco Leal, 387–419. Bogotá: Norma.

Campbell, Howard. 2010. *Drug War Zone: Frontline Dispatches from the Streets of El Paso and Juarez*. Austin: University of Texas Press.

Carothers, Tom, and Andreas E. Feldmann. 2021 (eds.). *Divisive Politics and Democratic Dangers in Latin America*. Washington, DC: Carnegie Endowment for International Peace.

Carrere, Michelle. 2022. "As Gangs Battle over Peru's Drug Trafficking Routes, Communities and Forest Are at Risk." *Mongabay News*, November 8. https://bit.ly/40DjqwQ.

Carvalho, Leandro S., and Rodrigo R. Soares. 2016. "Living on the Edge: Youth Entry, Career and Exit in Drug-Selling Gangs." *Journal of Economic Behavior & Organization* 121: 77–98.

Castells, Manuel. 2000. *The End of the Millenniuum*. 2nd ed. Oxford: Blackwell.

Cerna, Sarah, and Carlos Aníbal Peris. 2018. "Paraguay: La violencia como una cuestión de propiedad." In *Atlas de violencia en América Latina*, edited by Juan Mario Solís and Marcelo Moriconi, 420–53. San Luis Potosí: Universidad Autónoma de San Luis Potosí.

Chabat, Jorge. 2012. "Drug Trafficking and US–Mexico Relations." In *Mexico's Security Failure: Collapse into Criminal Violence*, edited by Mónica Serrano and Paul Kenny, 143–60. New York: Routledge.

Chehabi, Houchang E., and Juan Linz (eds). 1998. *Sultanistic Regimes*. Baltimore, MD: Johns Hopkins University Press.

Chill E., Pablo. 2018. "Shishigang." Online video clip. www.youtube.com/watch?v=BhFu-o1fKF4.

Clawson, Patrick, and Rensselear Lee. 1996. *The Andean Cocain Industry*. New York: Palgrave.

Comité Estadístico Interinstitucional de la Criminalidad. 2018. Homicidios en el Perú. www.inei.gob.pe/media/difusion/app/#p=4.

Corda, Alejandro, Ernesto Cortés, and Diego Piñol. 2019. *Cannabis en Latinoamérica: La ola verde y los retos hacia la regulación*. Washington Office for Latin America. www.wola.org/wp-content/uploads/2020/02/Cannabis-en-Latinoamérica-La-Ola-Verde.pdf.

Cotler, Julio. 1999. *Drogas y política en el Perú: La conexión norteamericana*. Lima: Insituto de Estudios Peruanos. https://repositorio.iep.org.pe/handle/IEP/679.

Courtwright, David T. 2019. *The Age of Addiction: How Bad Habits Became Big Business*. Cambridge, MA: Belknap Press of Harvard University Press.

Crenshaw, Martha. 1988. "Theories of Terrorism: Instrumental and Organizational Approaches." In *Inside Terrorist Organizations*, edited by David Rapoport, 13–31. New York: Columbia University Press.

Crouch, Colin. 2018. *The Globalization Backlash*. Cambridge: Polity.

Cruz, José Miguel. 2011. "Criminal Violence and Democratization in Central America: The Survival of the Violent State." *Latin American Politics and Society* 53 (4): 1–33.

Dalby, Chris. 2020. "Chile Sees Drug Trafficking as Most Severe National Security Threat: Survey." Insight Crime, June 3. https://insightcrime.org/news/analysis/chile-drug-trafficking-survey/.

2022. "Paraguay's Former President Losing Aura of Impunity." Insight Crime, October 24. https://insightcrime.org/news/paraguays-former-president-horacio-cartes-losing-aura-of-impunity/.

Dargent, Eduardo, Andreas E. Feldmann, and Juan Pablo Luna. 2017. "Greater State Capacity, Lesser Stateness: Lessons from the Peruvian Commodity Boom." *Politics and Society* 45 (1) 3–34.

Davis, Diane. 2006. "The Age of Insecurity: Violence and Social Disorder in the New Latin America." *Latin American Research Review* 41 (1): 179–91.

Davis, Diane, and Tina Hilgers. 2022. "The Pandemic and Organized Crime in Urban Latin America: New Sovereignty Arrangements or Business as Usual?" *Journal of Illicit Economies and Development* 4 (3): 241–56.

Dewey, Matías. 2012. "Illegal Police Protection and the Market for Stolen Vehicles in Buenos Aires." *Journal of Latin American Studies* 44 (4): 679–702.

2016. *El órden clandestino: Política, fuerzas de seguridad y mercados ilegales en la Argentina*. Buenos Aires: Katz Editores.

Dewey, Matías, Daniel Pedro Miguez, and Marcelo Fabián Saín. 2017. "The Strength of Collusion: A Conceptual Framework to Interpret Hybrid Social Orders." *Current Sociology* 65 (3): 395–410.

Donner, Richard F., and Ben Ross Schneider. 2016. "The Middle Income Trap: More Politics Than Economics." *World Politics* 68: 608–44.

Drummond, Ashley Day. 2008. "Coca, Cocaine and the International Regime against Drugs." *Law and Business Review of the Americas* 14 (1): 107–37.

Dudley, Steven, and Matt Taylor. 2020. "While Taking Paraguay–Brazil Border, PCC Tries to Control Its Own." Insight Crime, December 17. https://insightcrime.org/investigations/paraguay-brazil-border-pcc/.

Duncan, Gustavo. 2006. *Los señores de la guerra: De paramilitares, mafiosos y autodefensas en Colombia*. Bogotá: Planeta.

2015a. "Exclusión, insurrección y crímen." In *Contribución al entendimiento del conflicto armado en Colombia*, edited by Comisión Histórica del Conflicto y sus Víctimas, 249–94. Bogotá: Ediciones Desde Abajo.

2015b. *Más plata que plomo: El poder político del narcotráfico en Colombia y México*. Bogotá: Debate.

2022. *Beyond Plata o Plomo: Drugs and State Reconfiguration in Colombia*. Elements in Politics and Society in Latin America Series. New York: Cambridge University Press.

Durán-Martínez, Angélica. 2018. *The Politics of Drug Violence: Criminals, Cops and Politicians in Colombia and Mexico*. Oxford: Oxford University Press.

2021. "South America: From Acquiescence to Rebellion?" In *Transforming the War on Drugs: Warriors, Victims and Vulnerable Regions*, edited by Annette Idler and Juan Carlos Garzón, 133–60. Oxford: Oxford University Press.

Durand, Francisco. 2007. *El Perú fracturado: Formalidad, informalidad y economía delictiva*. Lima: Fondo Editorial Congreso del Perú.

Eaton, Kent. 2012. "The State in Latin America: Challenges, Challengers, Responses and Deficits." *Revista de Ciencia Política* 32 (3): 643–57.

EMOL. 2021. "Incautan un 751% más de drogas en la Araucanía y fiscal revela mayor producción local de marihuana," April 27. www.emol.com/noti cias/Nacional/2021/04/27/1019130/Drogas-La-Araucania.html.

Esberg, Jane. 2020. "More Than Cartels: Counting Mexico's Crime Rings." International Crisis Group. May 8. www.crisisgroup.org/latin-america-caribbean/mexico/more-cartels-counting-mexicos-crime-rings.

Expansión. 2020. "Uruguay: Homicidios Intencionales." https://datosmacro .expansion.com/demografia/homicidios/uruguay.

Felbab-Brown, Vanda. 2005. "The Coca Connection: Conflict and Drugs in Colombia and Peru." *Journal of Conflict Studies* 25 (2): 104–25.

Feldmann, Andreas E. 2019a. "Making Sense of Haiti's State Fragility and Violence: Combining Structure and Contingency." In *The Politics of Violence in Latin America*, edited by Pablo Policzer, 19–52. Calgary: University of Calgary Press.

2019b. "Colombia's Polarization Peace Efforts." In *Divided Democracy: The Global Challenge of Political Polarizations*, edited by Tom Carothers and Andrew O'Donohue, 153–74. Washington, DC: Brookings Institution Press.

Feldmann, Andreas E., and Juan Pablo Luna. 2022. "Criminal Governance and the Crisis of Contemporary Latin American States." *Annual Review of Sociology* 48 (1): 441–61.

Feltran, Gabriel. 2018. *Irmãos: Uma história do PCC*. São Paulo: Companhia das Letras.

Fernández Labbé, Marcos. 2009. "Del ficticio entusiasmo: El mercado de las drogas en el tránsito a la prohibición en Chile, 1920–1960." *Historia Crítica* 39: 62–83.

Flom, Hernán. 2022. *The Informal Regulation of Criminal Markets in Latin America*. Cambridge: Cambridge University Press.

Ford, Alessandro. 2022a. "Meth, Fentanyl, Ecstasy: Synthetic Drugs Flourish in Latin America." Insight Crime, September 12. https://insightcrime.org/news/meth-fentanyl-ecstasy-synthetic-drugs-flourish-in-latin-america/.

2022b. "Uruguay's Microtrafficking Approach Under Question as Homicides Jump." Insight Crime, May 20. https://insightcrime.org/news/uruguay-security-strategies-homicides-record-microtrafficking/.

Friman, Richard. 2009. "Drug Markets and the Selective Use of Violence." *Crime, Law and Social Change* 52 (3): 285–95.

Garat, Guillermo. 2016. *Paraguay: La tierra escondida. Exámen del mayor productor de cannabis de América del Sur*. Friedrich-Eberard-Stiftung, Bogotá. https://library.fes.de/pdf-files/bueros/la-seguridad/12809.pdf

Gieryn, Thomas F. 2000. "A Space for Place in Sociology." *Annual Review of Sociology* 26 (1): 463–96.

Gilman, Nils, Jesse Goldhammer, and Steven Weber. 2011. *Deviant Globalization: The Black Market in the 21st Century*. New York: Continuum.

Giraudy, Agustina, and Juan Pablo Luna. 2016. Unpacking the State's Uneven Territorial Reach: Evidence from Latin America. In *States in the Developing World*, edited by Miguel Angel Centeno, Atul Kolhi, and Deborah Yashar, 85–108. New York: Cambridge University Press.

Giraudy, Agustina, Eduardo Moncada, and Richard Snyder (eds.). 2019. *Inside Countries: Subnational Research in Comparative Politics*. New York: Cambridge University Press.

Glave, Manuel, and Cristina Rosemberg. 2005. *La comercialización de la hoja de coca en el Perú*. Grupo de Análisis para el Desarrollo, Lima. https://pdf.usaid.gov/pdf_docs/PNADD346.pdf.

González, Yanilda María. 2017. "'What Citizens Can See of the State': Police and the Construction of Democratic Citizenship in Latin America." *Theoretical Criminology* 21 (4): 494–511.

Gootenberg, Paul. 2003. "Between Coca and Cocaine: A Century or More of U.S.–Peruvian Drug Paradoxes, 1860–1980." *Hispanic American Historical Review* 83 (1): 120–50.

2007. "The 'Pre-Colombian' Era of Drug Trafficking in the Americas: Cocaine, 1947–1965." *The Americas* 64 (2): 133–76.

2008. *Andean Cocaine: The Making of a Global Drug*. Chapel Hill: University of North Carolina Press.

2021. "Building the Global Drug Regime: Origins and Impact, 1909–1990s." In *Transforming the War on Drugs: Warriors, Victims and Vulnerable*

Regions, edited by Annette Idler and Juan Carlos Garzón, 53–82. Oxford: Oxford University Press.

Grillo, Ioan. 2015. "Mexican Cartels: A Century of Defying U.S. Drug Policy." *Brown Journal of World Affairs* 20 (1): 253–65.

Grisaffi, Thomas, Linda Farthing, Kathryn Ledebur, Maritza Paredes, and Álvaro Pastor. 2021. "From Criminals to Citizens: The Applicability of Bolivia's Community-Based Coca Control Policy to Peru." *World Development* 146: 2–14.

Guarello, Juan Cristóbal. 2021. *País barrabrava*. Santiago: Debate.

Guzmán, Juan Andrés. 2020. "Juan Pablo Luna: Se desmanteló la idea de que Chile tenía una gran capacidad estatal de establecer órden." *CIPER Chile*, March 12. https://bit.ly/3HCzclh.

Hallam, Christopher, and David Bewley-Taylor. 2021. "The International Drug Control Regime: Crisis and Fragmentation." In *Transforming the War on Drugs: Warriors, Victims and Vulnerable Regions*, edited by Annete Idler and Juan Carlos Garzón, 83–112. Oxford: Oxford University Press.

Hellman, Joel S., Geraint Jones, and Daniel Kauffmann. 2013. "Seize the State, Seize the Day: State Capture, Corruption, and Influence in Transition." World Bank Working Paper 2444. https://doi.org/10.1596/1813-9450-2444.

Herbst, Jeffrey. 2000. *States and Power in Africa: Comparative Lessons in Authority and Control*. Princeton, NJ: Princeton University Press.

Hirschman, Albert O. 1958. *The Strategy of Economic Development*. New Haven, CT: Yale University Press.

Hobbs, Dick. 1998. "Going Down the Glocal: The Local Context of Organised Crime." *Howard Journal of Criminal Justice* 37 (4): 407–22.

Holland, Alisha C. 2017. *Forbearance as Redistribution: The Politics of Informal Welfare in Latin America*. Cambridge: Cambridge University Press.

Holligan, Anna. 2019. "Is the Netherlands Becoming a Narco-State?" *BBC News*, December 19. www.bbc.com/news/world-europe-50821542.

Holmes, Jennifer S., and Sheila Amin Gutiérrez de Piñeres. 2006. "The Illegal Drug Industry, Violence and the Colombian Economy: A Department Level Analysis." *Bulletin of Latin American Research* 25 (1): 104–18.

Huguet, Clarissa, and Ilona Szabó de Carvalho. 2008. "Violence in the Brazilian Favelas and the Role of the Police." *New Directons in Youth Development* 119: 93–109.

Idler, Annette. 2019. *Borderland Battles: Violence, Crime, and Governance at the Edges of Colombia's War*. Oxford: Oxford University Press.

——. 2021. Warriors, Victims and Vulnerable Regions: A Critical Perspective on the War on Drugs. In *Transforming the War on Drugs: Warriors, Victims and Vulnerable Regions*, edited by Annette Idler and Juan Carlos Garzón, 19–49. Oxford: Oxford University Press.

Ignacio, Yordano. 2018. "Mambo Para Los Presos." Online video clip. www.youtube.com/watch?v=hfKjUEx-6bY.

Infobae. 2022. "Cedro advierte que el consumo de drogas se ha incrementado en 15% en el Perú," August 17. https://bit.ly/3AthxYX.

Informe Especial. 2019. "Los Risas, el salvaje y poderoso clan narco." Televisión Nacional de Chile, April 7. Online video clip. https://bit.ly/3B011Qp.

Inkster, Nigel, and Virginia Comolli. 2012. *Drugs Insecurity and Failed States: The Problems of Prohibition*. London: Routledge (for the International Institute for Strategic Studies).

Insight Crime. 2018. "Uruguay Profile." https://insightcrime.org/uruguay-organized-crime-news/uruguay/.

2020. "First Capital Command – PCC." https://insightcrime.org/brazil-organized-crime-news/first-capital-command-pcc.

2021a. "All About Colombia Groups." https://insightcrime.org/tag/colombia-groups/page/2/.

2021b. "Amambay Paraguay," February 25. https://insightcrime.org/paraguay-organized-crime-news/amambay-paraguay/.

2022. "Red Command." https://insightcrime.org/brazil-organized-crime-news/red-command-profile/.

Instituto Nacional de Derechos Humanos. 2021. *Estado de Chile y pueblo mapuche: Análisis de tendencia en materia de violencia estatal*. https://bit.ly/42hFyyn.

Inter-American Drug Abuse Control Commission. 2013. *The Drug Problem in the Americas: Studies. The Economics of Drug Trafficking*. Organization of American States. www.cicad.oas.org/drogas/elinforme/informedrogas2013/laeconomicanarcotrafico_eng.pdf.

Jensen, Michael C., and William H. Meckling. 1976. "Theory of the Firm: Managerial Behavior, Agency Costs and Ownership Structure." *Journal of Financial Economics* 3 (4): 305–60.

Jones, Katie. 2021. Killings Pile Up in Uruguay Due to Brazil Gang War. Insight Crime, August 24. https://insightcrime.org/news/killings-pile-up-uruguay-brazil-gang-war/.

Juetersonke, Oliver, Robert Muggah, and Dennis Rogers. 2009. "Gangs, Urban Violence, and Security Interventions in Central America." *Security Dialogue* 40 (4–5): 373–97.

Kaldor, Mary. 2001. *New and Old Wars*. Stanford, CA: Stanford University Press.

Kalyvas, Stathis. 2015. "How Civil Wars Help Explain Organized Crime – and How They Do Not." *Journal of Conflict Resolution* 59 (8): 15–40.

Kan, Paul Rexton. 2016. *Drug Trafficking and International Security*. Boulder, CO: Rowman & Littlefield.

Keen, David. 1996. *The Economic Functions of Violence in Civil Wars*. Oxford: Oxford University Press (for the International Institute for Strategic Studies).

Knight, Alan. 2012. "Narco-Violence and the State in Modern Mexico." In *Violence, Coercion and State Making in Twentieth Century Mexico: The Other Half of the Centaur*, edited by Wil Pansters, 115–34. Stanford, CA: Stanford University Press.

Koonings, Kees. 2012. "New Violence, Insecurity and the State: Comparative Reflections on Latin America and Mexico." In *Violence, Coercion and State-Making in Twentieth Century Mexico: The Other Half of the Centaur*, edited by Wil Pansters, 255–78. Stanford, CA: Stanford University Press.

La Diaria. 2022. "El Caso Astesiano." https://ladiaria.com.uy/seccion/el-caso-astesiano/.

Ladra, Antonio. 2014. *Narcos: Lilo, Clavijo, Bocha y la operación campanita en el Uruguay*. Montevideo: Editorial Sudamericana.

Latin American Commission on Drugs and Democracy. 2020. *Drugs and Democracy: Towards a Paradigm Shift*. www.globalcommissionondrugs.org/wp-content/uploads/2016/06/drugs-and-democracy_book_EN.pdf.

Leal, Gustavo. 2021. *Historias de sicarios en Uruguay*. Montevideo: Debate.

Leiva, Ricardo. 2008. "La ruta clandestina del oro y la plata." Canal 180 podcast. www.180.com.uy/articulo/178_La-ruta-clandestina-del-oro-y-la-plata.

Lessing, Benjamin. 2015. "Logic of Violence in Criminal War." *Journal of Conflict Resolution* 59 (8): 486–516.

2017. *Making Peace in Drug Wars: Crackdowns and Cartels in Latin America*. Cambridge: Cambridge University Press.

2021. "Conceptualizing Criminal Governance." *Perspectives on Politics* 19 (3): 854–73.

2022. "Governança criminal na América Latina em perspectiva comparada: Apresentação à edição especial." *Revista de Estudos de Conflito e Controle Social* 15: 1–10.

Levine, Harry G. 2003. "Global Drug Prohibition: Its Uses and Crises." *International Journal of Drug Policy* 14 (2): 145–53.

Levy, Jack S. 2008. "Case Studies: Types, Designs, and Logics of Inference." *Conflict Managment and Peace Studies*, 25 (1): 1–18.

Lissardy, Gerardo. 2019. Uruguay: Cuánto ha cambiado realmente el mercado de las drogas en el País con la legalización de la marihuana. BBC News Mundo, December 19. www.bbc.com/mundo/noticias-america-latina-50667423.

Llorente, María Victoria, and Jeremy McDermott. 2014. "Colombia's Lessons for Mexico." In *One Goal, Two Struggles: Confronting Crime and Violence in Colombia and Mexico*, edited by Cynthia Arnson, Eric Olson, and Christian Zaino, 1–37. Reports on the Americas No. 32, Woodrow Wilson Center, Washington, DC. https://bit.ly/3ATXLGk.

Loweman, Brian (ed.). 2006. *Addicted to Failure: U.S. Security Policy in Latin America and the Andean Region*. Boulder, CO: Rowman & Littlefield.

Luna, Juan Pablo. 2021. *La chusma inconsciente: La crisis de un país atendido por sus propios dueños*. Santiago: Catalonia.

Luna, Juan Pablo, Rafael Piñeiro, Fernando Rosenblatt, and Gabriel Vommaro (eds.). 2021. *Diminished Parties: Democratic Representation in Contemporary Latin America*. New York: Cambridge University Press.

Luneke, Alejandra. 2021. "Narcotráfico: Escuchando Las Prioridades Desde Los 'Barrios Críticos'." *CIPER Chile*, March 6. www.ciperchile.cl/2021/03/06/narcotrafico-escuchando-las-prioridades-desde-los-barrios-criticos/.

Lupsha, Peter. 1983. "Networks versus Networking: Analysis of an Organized Crime Group." In *Career Criminals*, edited by Gordon P. Waldo, 59–87. Beverly Hills, CA: Sage Publications.

Magaloni, Beatriz, Gustavo Robles, Aila M. Matanock, Alberto Díaz-Cayeros, and Vidal Romero. 2020. "Living in Fear: The Dynamics of Extortion in Mexico's Drug War." *Comparative Political Studies* 53 (7): 1124–74.

Mahoney, James. 2010. *Colonialism and Postcolonial Development: Spanish America in Comparative Perspective*. Cambridge: Cambridge University Press.

Mainwaring, Scott, and Aníbal Pérez-Liñán. 2013. *Democracies and Dictatorships in Latin America: Emergence, Survival and Fall*. Cambridge: Cambridge University Press.

Mantilla, Jorge, and Andreas E. Feldmann. 2021. "Criminal Governance in Latin America." In *The Oxford Encyclopedia of International Criminology*, edited by Edna Eretz and Peter Ibarra, 212–32. Oxford: Oxford University Press.

Matus, Alejandra. 1999. *El libro negro de la justicia chilena*. Santiago: Planeta.

May, Channing. 2017. *Transnational Crime and the Developing World*. Global Financial Integrity, Washington, DC. https://gfintegrity.org/report/transnational-crime-and-the-developing-world/.

Mazzuca, Sebastián L., and Gerardo L. Munck. 2021. *A Middle-Quality Institutional Trap: Democracy and State Capacity in Latin America*.

Elements in Politics and Society in Latin America Series. New York: Cambridge University Press.

McAllister, William B. 2012. *Reflections on a Century of International Drug Control*. LSE Ideas Special Report, London School of Economics and Political Science. http://eprints.lse.ac.uk/47122/1/Governingtheglobal drugwars%28published%29.pdf.

McClintock, Cynthia. 1988. "The War on Drugs: The Peruvian Case." *Journal of Interamerican Studies and World Affairs* 30 (2–3): 127–42.

2005. "The Evolution of Internal War in Peru: The Conjunction of Need, Creed, and Organizational Finance." In *Rethinking the Economics of War*, edited by Cynthia Arnson and William Zartman, 52–83. Baltimore, MD and Washington, DC: The Johns Hopkins University Press and the Woodrow Wilson Center Press.

Méndez, Juan, Guillermo O'Donnell, and Paulo Sergio Pinheiro. 1996. *The (Un)Rule of Law and the Underprivileged in Latin America*. Notre Dame, IN: University of Notre Dame Press.

Migdal, Joel. 2001. *State in Society: Studying How States and Societies Transform and Constitute One Another*. Cambridge: Cambridge University Press.

Moncada, Eduardo. 2016. *Cities, Business, and the Politics of Urban Violence in Latin America*. Palo Alto, CA: Stanford University Press.

2022. *Resisting Extortion: Victims, Criminals, and States in Latin America*. Cambridge: Cambridge University Press.

Montenegro, Santiago, Jorge Llano, and Diana Ibañez. 2019. *El PIB de la cocaína 2005–2018: Una estimación empírica*. Documentos CEDE Universidad de los Andes, Colombia. https://repositorio.uniandes.edu.co/handle/1992/41108.

Moriconi, Marcelo, and Carlos Aníbal Peris. 2019. "Merging Legality with Illegality in Paraguay: The Cluster of Order in Pedro Juan Caballero." *Third World Quarterly* 40 (12): 2210–27.

2022. "Cultivating Cannabis in a Paraguayan Nature Reserve: Incentives and Moral Justification for Breaking the Law." *Trends in Organized Crime*. https://doi.org/10.1007/s12117-022-09464-z.

Mortimer, Golden W. 2000. *History of Coca: The Divine Plant of the Incas*. 3rd ed. Honolulu, HI: University Press of the Pacific.

Muggah, Robert, and Steven Dudley. 2021. "COVID-19 Is Reconfiguring Organized Crime in Latin America." *Small Wars Journal*, February 3. https://smallwarsjournal.com/jrnl/art/covid-19-reconfiguring-organized-crime-latin-america-and-caribbean.

Muñoz, Paula. 2021. "Peru's Democracy in Search of Representation." In *Divisive Politics and Democratic Dangers in Latin America*, edited by

Tom Carothers and Andreas E. Feldmann, 27–31. Carnegie Endowment for International Peace, Washignton, DC.

Nadelmann, Ethan A. 1990. "Global Prohibition Regimes: The Evolution of Norms in International Society." *International Organization* 44 (4): 479–526.

Natarajan, Mangai. 2019. "Drug Trafficking." In *International and Transnational Crime and Justice*, edited by Mangai Natarajan, 5–11. New York: Cambridge University Press.

Natarajan, Mangai, Marco Zanella, and Christopher Yu. 2015. "Classifying the Variety of Drug Trafficking Organizations." *Journal of Drug Issues* 45 (4): 409–30.

Newman, Lucía. 2021. "A Journey through Chile's Conflict with Mapuche Rebel Groups." *Al Jazeera*, April 12. www.aljazeera.com/features/2021/ 4/12/a-journey-through-chiles-conflict-with-mapuche-resistance-groups.

O'Donnell, Guillermo. 1993. "On the State, Democratization and Some Conceptual Problems: A Latin American View with Some Glances at Post Communist Countries." *World Development* 21 (8): 1355–69.

Obando, Enrique. 2006. "US Policy toward Peru: At Odds for 20 Years." In *Addicted to Failure: US Security Policy in Latin America and the Andean Region*, edited by Brian Loveman, 169–96. Lanham, MD: Rowman & Littlefield.

Office of Drug Control Policy. 2021. "ONDCP Releases Data on Coca Cultivation and Potential Cocaine Production in the Andean Region." The White House, July 16. https://bit.ly/41CDRLZ.

Organization of American States. 2020. *Informe sobre el consumo de drogas en Las Américas.* http://cicad.oas.org/Main/ssMain/HTML%20REPORT% 20DRUG%202019/mobile/index.html.

Osorno, Diego. 2009. *El Cartel de Sinaloa: Una historia del uso político del narco.* Mexico City: Grijalbo.

Pacheco, Elyssa. 2012. "The Evolution of the Drug Trade in Peru's Cocaine Heartland." Insight Crime, August 31. https://insightcrime.org/news/ana lysis/the-evolution-of-the-drug-trade-in-perus-cocaine-heartland/.

Pansters, Wil. 2018. "Drug Trafficking, the Informal Order, and Caciques. Reflections on the Crime–Governance Nexus in Mexico." *Global Crime* 19 (3–4): 315–38.

Paredes, Maritza, and Hernán Manrique. 2021. "The State's Developmentalist Illusion and the Origins of Illegal Coca Cultivation in Peru's Alto Huallaga Valley (1960–80)." *Journal of Latin American Studies* 53 (2): 245–67.

Pechinski, Ashley. 2021. "Weapons Traffickers Target Chile's Port of Iquique." Insight Crime, August 6. https://insightcrime.org/news/smuggled-weap ons-cause-concern-chile.

Penglase, Ben. 2008. "The Bastard Child of the Dictatorship: The Comando Vermelho and the Birth of 'Narco-Culture' in Rio de Janeiro." *Luso Brasilian Review* 45 (1): 118–45.

Policzer, Pablo. 2009. *The Rise and Fall of Repression in Chile*. Notre Dame, IN: University of Notre Dame Press.

Queirolo, Rosario, Cecilia Rossel, Eliana Álvarez, and Lorena Repetto. 2019. "Why Uruguay Legalized Marihuana? The Open Window of Public Insecurity." *Addiction* 114 (7): 1313–21.

Radwin, Max. 2020a. "Paraguay Shakes Up Drug Policy with First Medical Cannabis Licenses." Insight Crime, March 16. https://insightcrime.org/news/brief/paraguay-medical-cannabis.

———. 2020b. "Tensions Rise in Bolivia's Chapare As Government Escalates Anti-Drug Operations." Insight Crime, May 8. https://insightcrime.org/news/analysis/bolivia-chapare-drug-operations.

Rainsford, Cat, and Sergio Saffon. 2022. "Gigantesca operación antidrogas arroja luz sobre narcopolítica en Paraguay." Insight Crime, March 7. https://es.insightcrime.org/noticias/gigantesca-operacion-antidrogas-arroja-luz-narcopolitica-paraguay/.

Retberg, Angelika. 2021. "From Old Battles to New Challenges in Colombia." In *Divisive Politics and Democratic Dangers in Latin America*, edited by Tom Carothers and Andreas E. Feldmann, 18–21. Carnegie Endowment for International Peace, Washington, DC.

Reuter, Peter. 2009. "Systemic Violence in Drug Markets." *Crime, Law and Social Change* 52 (3): 275–84.

Reuter, Peter, and Michael Tonry. 2020. "Organized Crime: Less Than Meets the Eye." *Crime and Justice* 49: 1–16.

Rosen, Jonathan D. 2014. *The Losing War: Plan Colombia and Beyond*. Albany: State University of New York Press.

Ross, Stephen A. 1973. "The Economic Theory of Agency: The Principal's Problem." *American Economic Review* 63 (2): 134–39.

Rotberg, Robert I. (ed.). 2003. *State Failure and State Weakness in a Time of Terror*. Washington, DC: Brookings Institution Press.

Rotker, Susana (ed.). 2002. *Citizens of Fear: Urban Violence in Latin America*. New Brunswick, NJ: Rutgers University Press.

Roy, King, and Bruna Valensia. 2014. "Power, Control, and Symbiosis in Brazilian Prisons." *South Atlantic Quarterly* 113 (3): 503–28.

Saffón, Sergio. 2020. "Paraguay lidia con ostentoso retorno de una vieja amenaza criminal." Insight Crime, September 22. https://es.insightcrime.org/noticias/analisis/paraguay-retorno-amenaza-criminal/.

Saín, Marcelo. 2002. *El leviatán azul: Policía y política en la Argentina*. Buenos Aires: Siglo XXI.

Salazar, Manuel. 2019. "La historia de la narcopolítica en Chile." *Interferencia*, June 30. https://interferencia.cl/articulos/la-historia-de-la-narcopolitica-en-chile.

Sampó, Carolina, and Valeska Troncoso. 2022. "Cocaine Trafficking from Non-Traditional Ports: Examining the Cases of Argentina, Chile and Uruguay." *Trends in Organized Crime*. https://doi.org/10.1007/s12117-021-09441-y.

Schlichte, Klaus. 2009. *In the Shadow of Violence: The Politics of Armed Groups*. Frankfurt: Campus Verlag.

Schoultz, Lars. 1999. *Beneath the United States: A History of US Policy towards Latin America*. Cambridge, MA: Harvard University Press.

Sepúveda, Nicolás, and ABC Color. 2022. "Cita en Paraguay: Luksic se reunió con el ex-presidente Cartes, su socio acusado por EE.UU de corrupción y vínculos con el terrorismo." *CIPER Chile*, August 7. https://bit.ly/3AvvjKF.

Shelley, Louise. 2005. "The Unholy Trinity: Transnational Crime, Corruption and Terrorism." *Brown Journal of International Affairs* XI (2): 101–11.

    2014. *Dirty Entanglements: Corruption, Crime and Terrorism*. Cambridge: Cambridge University Press.

Shirk, David, and Joel Wallman. 2015. "Understanding Mexico's Drug Violence." *Journal of Conflict Resolution* 59 (8): 1348–76.

Shuldiner, Henry. 2022. "Paraguay May Be Shifting from Producing LSD and MDMA to Consuming Them." Insight Crime, 10 June. https://insight crime.org/news/paraguay-lsd-mdma-producing-consuming/.

Sibila, Deborah A., and Andrea J. Weiss. 2014. "Narco Culture." In *The Encyclopedia of Theoretical Criminology*, edited by Mitchell Miller, 1–4. London: Wiley-Blackwell.

Sicilia, Javier. 2016. *El deshabitado*. Mexico City: Grijalbo.

Simon, José Luis. 1992. "Drug Addiction and Trafficking in Paraguay: An Approach to the Problem during the Transition." *Journal of Interamerican Studies and World Affairs* 34 (3): 155–200.

Slater, Dan, and Diana Kim. 2015. "Standoffish States: Nonliterate Leviathans in Southeast Asia." *Trans-Regional and National Studies of Southeast Asia* 3 (1): 25–44.

Smilde, David, Verónica Zubillaga, and Rebecca Hanson (eds.). 2022. *The Paradox of Violence in Venezuela: Crime and Revolution*. Pittsburgh, PA: Pittsburgh University Press.

Smith, Amy Erica, and Taylor C. Boas. 2020. "Religion, Sexuality Politics, and the Transformation of Latin American Electorates." Paper delivered at the

Annual Meeting of the American Political Science Association, September 10–13. www.ucis.pitt.edu/clas/sites/default/files/Smith%20Boas%202020%20Charlemos.pdf.

Snyder, Richard, and Angelica Durán-Martínez. 2009. "Does Illegality Breed Violence? Drug Trafficking and State Sponsored Protection Rackets." *Crime, Law and Social Change* 52: 253–73.

Soifer, Hillel. 2013. "State Power and the Economic Origins of Democracy." *Studies in Comparative International Development* 48 (1): 1–22.

Solar, Carlos. 2018. *Government and Governance of Security: The Politics of Organised Crime in Chile*. London: Routledge.

Solis, Juan Mario, Sarah Cerna, and Carlos Aníbal Peris. 2017. "¿Qué explica la violencia letal en Paraguay? Un estudio con intención." *Perfiles Latinoamericanos* 27 (53): 1–26.

Strange, Susan. 1996. *The Retreat of the State: The Diffusion of Power in the World Economy*. Cambridge: Cambridge University Press.

Svampa, Maristella. 2019. *Las fronteras del neoextractivismo En América Latina: Conflictos socioambientales, giro ecoterritorial y nuevas dependencias*. Guadalajara: CALAS.

Sverdlick, Ana R. 2005. "Terrorists and Organized Crime Entrepreneurs in the 'Triple Frontier' among Argentina, Brazil, and Paraguay." *Trends in Organized Crime* 9 (2): 84–93.

Televisión Nacional de Chile. 2021. "La huella del temido Cartel de Juárez en Chile." Online video clip. www.youtube.com/watch?v=2sNM8gyawv8.

Tennenbaum, Gabriel. 2018. "El mercado de las drogas ilegales en Uruguay." *Revista Mexicana de Sociología* 80 (4): 855–80.

Thoumi, Francisco. 2003. *Illegal Drugs, Economy, and Society in the Andes*. Washington, DC: Woodrow Wilson Center.

2016. *Drogas ilegales y economía en los Andes*. Bogotá: Confederación de Adolescencia y Juventud de América Latina y El Caribe.

Transnational Institute. 2006. "El paco bajo la lupa: El mercado de pasta base de cocaína en el Cono Sur," October 1. www.tni.org/es/publicacion/el-paco-bajo-la-lupa.

Transparency International. 2020. "Corruption Perception Index 2020." www.transparency.org/en/cpi/2020.

Trejo, Guillermo, and Sandra Ley. 2017. "Why Did Drug Cartels Go to War in Mexico? Subnational Party Alternation, the Breakdown of Criminal Protection, and the Onset of Large-Scale Violence." *Comparative Political Studies* 51 (7): 900–37.

2020. *Votes, Drugs and Violence: The Political Logic of Criminal Wars in Mexico*. New York: Cambridge University Press.

UC San Diego. 2021. *Organized Crime and Violence in Mexico: 2020 Special Report*. Justice in Mexico Project, Department of Political Science & International Relations. https://justiceinmexico.org/wp-content/uploads/2020/07/OCVM-2020.pdf.

United Nations Development Programme. 2013. *Citizen Secuity with a Human Face: Evidence and Proposals for Latin America*. https://hdr.undp.org/content/citizen-security-human-face.

Ungar, Brigitte. 2007. *The Scale and Impacts of Money Laundering*. Northhampton, MA: Edward Elgar.

United Nations Office on Drugs and Crime. 2011. *Estimating Illicit Financial Flows Resulting from Drug Trafficking and Other Transnational Organized Crimes*. www.unodc.org/documents/data-and-analysis/Studies/Illicit_financial_flows_2011_web.pdf.

  2020. *World Drug Report*. https://wdr.unodc.org/wdr2020/en/cross-cutting.html.

  2021. World Drug Report. www.unodc.org/unodc/en/data-and-analysis/wdr2021.html.

  2022. World Drug Report. www.unodc.org/unodc/data-and-analysis/world-drug-report-2022.html.

Uribe, Andrés, Benjamin Lessing, Noah Shouela, Elayne Stecher, and Douglas Block. 2022. "Criminal Governance in Latin America: An Initial Assessment of Its Extent and Correlates." SSRN Papers. http://dx.doi.org/10.2139/ssrn.4302432.

Varese, Federico. 2017. "What Is Organised Crime?" In *Redefining Organised Crime: A Challenge for the European Union*, edited by Stefania Carnevale, Serena Forlati, and Orsetta Giolo, 27–53. Oxford: Hart Publishing.

Vilalta, Carlos. 2020. "Violence in Latin America: An Overview of Research and Issues." *Annual Review of Sociology* 46: 693–706.

Von Lampe, Klaus. 2012. "Transnational Organized Crime Challenges for Future Research." *Crime, Law and Social Change* 58 (2): 179–94.

  2016. *Organized Crime. Analyzing Illegal Activities, Criminal Structures, and Extra-Legal Governance*. Thousand Oaks, CA: Sage Publications.

Williams, Phil. 2001. "Transnational Criminal Networks." In *Networks and Netwars: The Future of Terror, Crime, and Militancy*, edited by John Arquilla and John Ronfeldt, 61–98. Los Angeles, CA: Rand Corporation.

  2016. "Illicit Threats: Organized Crime, Drugs, Small Arms." In *Routledge Handbook of Latin American Security*, edited by Arie Kacowicz and David Mares, 266–76. New York: Routledge.

Willis, Graham Denyer. 2015. *The Killing Consensus: Police, Organized Crime, and the Regulation of Life and Death in Urban Brazil*. Berkeley: University of California Press.

World Population Review. 2023. "Incarceration Rates by Country." https://worldpopulationreview.com/country-rankings/incarceration-rates-by-country.

Yashar, Deborah. 2018. *Homicidal Ecologies: Illicit Economies and Complicit States in Latin America*. Cambridge: Cambridge University Press.

Zarazaga, Rodrigo. 2014. "Brokers beyond Clientelism: A New Perspective through the Argentine Case." *Latin American Politics and Society* 56 (3): 23–45.

Acknowledgments

We thank Juan Albarracín, Ana Arjona, Gustavo Duncan, Gustavo Leal, Benjamin Lessing, Dipali Mukhopadhyay, Gonzalo Parra, Rachel Beatty Riedl, Fernando Rosenblatt, Carolina Sampó, and Ben Ross Schneider for their generous and insightful feedback on several iterations of this Element and for their encouragement and support. We acknowledge critical research and editorial assistance from Antonia Brown, Renata Boada, Jorge Mantilla, Mariene Rodríguez, David Schwartz, Matt Seidel, and members of the *Instituto Milenio para el Estudio de la Democracia y Violencia* who participated in a special workshop in Santiago de Chile in November 2022. We also relied on a list of interviews for the Chilean case kindly made available by Pilar Larroulet. We also acknowledge the support of Sara Doskow and Rachel Blaifeder at CUP.

This work was funded by the ANID – Millenium Initiative Program – ICS2019_025 (VIODEMOS) and IMFD-Chile. The project also received generous funding from ANID –FONDECYT Project #1190345 – and from the Center of Applied Ecology and Sustainability (CAPES), ANID PIA/BASAL FB0002. Juan Pablo Luna is a 2023 Harry Frank Gughenheim Distinguished Scholar, and he has received generous funding from the Harry Frank Gughenheim Foundation during the completion of this work. Andreas E. Feldmann acknowledges the support of the UIC College of Liberal Arts and Sciences, the International Development Research Centre (IDRC), and the Carnegie Endowment for International Peace.

Cambridge Elements ≡

Politics of Development

Rachel Beatty Riedl

Einaudi Center for International Studies and Cornell University

Rachel Beatty Riedl is the Director and John S. Knight Professor of the Einaudi Center for International Studies and Professor in the Government Department and School of Public Policy at Cornell University. Riedl is the author of the award-winning *Authoritarian Origins of Democratic Party Systems in Africa* (2014) and co-author of *From Pews to Politics: Religious Sermons and Political Participation in Africa* (with Gwyneth McClendon, 2019). She studies democracy and institutions, governance, authoritarian regime legacies, and religion and politics in Africa. She serves on the Editorial Committee of *World Politics* and the Editorial Board of *African Affairs, Comparative Political Studies, Journal of Democracy,* and *Africa Spectrum.* She is co-host of the podcast Ufahamu Africa.

Ben Ross Schneider

Massachusetts Institute of Technology

Ben Ross Schneider is Ford International Professor of Political Science at MIT and Director of the MIT-Brazil program. Prior to moving to MIT in 2008, he taught at Princeton University and Northwestern University. His books include *Business Politics and the State in 20th Century Latin America* (2004), *Hierarchical Capitalism in Latin America* (2013), *Designing Industrial Policy in Latin America: Business–Government Relations and the New Developmentalism* (2015), and *New Order and Progress: Democracy and Development in Brazil* (2016). He has also written on topics such as economic reform, democratization, education, labor markets, inequality, and business groups.

Advisory Board

Yuen Yuen Ang, *University of Michigan*
Catherine Boone, *London School of Economics*
Melani Cammett, *Harvard University* (former editor)
Stephan Haggard, *University of California, San Diego*
Prerna Singh, *Brown University*
Dan Slater, *University of Michigan*

About the series

The Element series *Politics of Development* provides important contributions on both established and new topics on the politics and political economy of developing countries. A particular priority is to give increased visibility to a dynamic and growing body of social science research that examines the political and social determinants of economic development, as well as the effects of different development models on political and social outcomes.

Cambridge Elements $\equiv$

Politics of Development

Printed in the United States
by Baker & Taylor Publisher Services